ANCIENT CIVILISATIONS OF BASILICATA
TREASURES EMERGING TO LIGHT

edited by
Angelo Bottini, Annamaria Mauro, Massimo Osanna

«L'ERMA» di BRETSCHNEIDER
Roma-Bristol (USA)

ANCIENT CIVILISATIONS OF BASILICATA.
TREASURES EMERGING TO LIGHT

Athens, Acropolis Museum, Temporary Exhibition Gallery
October 18, 2024 - January 26, 2025

Created and promoted by

MINISTRY OF CULTURE - Italy

Minister
Alessandro Giuli

GENERAL DIRECTORATE MUSEUMS - Italy

Director General Museums
Massimo Osanna

Service II - "National Museum System and Promotion of Cultural Heritage"
Roberto Vannata

Service III - "Exploitation and Communication of Cultural Heritage"
Luca Mercuri

Exhibition curated by
Massimo Osanna e Annamaria Mauro

Project managers
Lara Anniboletti
Elisabetta Scungio

Information panels
Angelo Bottini
Laura D'Esposito

**NATIONAL MUSEUMS OF MATERA
REGIONAL DIRECTORATE NATIONAL
MUSEUMS OF BASILICATA**

Director
Annamaria Mauro

Supported by

Exhibition Office
Laura D'Esposito
Adriana Sciacovelli
Lorena Trivigno

Tender and Contracts Office
Francesca Cirrottola
Claudio Fortunato
Monica Vassallo

Press and Communication Office
Vittoria Fonsa
Letizia Montagnuolo

Layout design
Vincenzo De Luce

Conservation and Restoration
Consorzio Kavaklik Restauro
Studio Malincaia. Conservazione e restauro di opere d'arte

Exhibition displays
IDM S.r.l.

Graphics
Areablu Edizioni S.r.l.

Transportation
De Marinis S.r.l.

Translations
Language Academy
Lydia Trakatelli

Insurance
GT Insurance

Lending Museums

National Museums of Matera "D. Ridola" Museum

National Archaeological Museum of Metaponto

National Archaeological Museum of the Siritide – Policoro

Exhibition catalogue edited by
Angelo Bottini
Annamaria Mauro
Massimo Osanna

Editorial Coordination
Lara Anniboletti
Laura D'Esposito

Essays by
Angelo Bottini
Annamaria Mauro
Massimo Osanna
Nikolaos Chr. Stampolidis

Catalogue entries edited by
Addolorata Preite

In collaboration with
Carmelo Colelli
Vincenzo Cracolici
Laura D'Esposito

Photographic records
Adam Oleksiak/G-M Studio
Fotografia di beni culturali-archivio dell'arte.
Pedicini Fotografi

ACROPOLIS MUSEUM

General Director
Professor Nikolaos Chr. Stampolidis

Supported by

Exhibitions office
Anna Vlachaki
Mariangela Ielo

Press and Communication Office
Danae Zaoussi
Aggelos Koropoulis
Aliki Lampropoulos

Conservation Department
Constantinos Vasiliadis

Editing translations
Anna Vlachaki

Constructions
Antonis Giannakidis – No Limits Constructions

Construction supervision
George Karagiorgos

Directorate of Visitor Services
Sofia Stavropoulou

Directorate of Technical Services
Panagiotis Kritsikis

Security Department
Athanasios Mandas

Ministero degli Affari Esteri
e della Cooperazione Internazionale

**MINISTRY OF FOREIGN AFFAIRS
AND INTERNATIONAL COOPERATION**

Minister and Vice-President of the Council of Ministers
Antonio Tajani

Directorate General for Public and Cultural Diplomacy

Director General
Alessandro De Pedys

Deputy Director General for Public and Cultural Diplomacy
Central Director for the Promotion of Italian Culture and Language
Min. Filippo La Rosa

Unit for the Coordination of Italian Cultural Institutes
Unit Head
Cons. Amb. Marco Maria Cerbo

Project Manager
Nicoletta Di Blasi

Italian Cultural Institute of Athens
Direttore Francesco Neri

Nikolaos Chr. Stampolidis
Director General of the Acropolis Museum

Once again the excellent collaboration that has been established between Greece and Italy in culture bore its richest fruits.

The exhibition "Ancient civilisations of Basilicata. Treasures emerging to light", organized by the General Directorate of Museums of Italy and the network of Basilicata Museums, is inaugurated in a complete form at the Acropolis Museum.

Through this exhibition, the relationship of the early civilization of Basilicata and the contact with the Greeks and the ancient Greek civilization in the territory that was to become the Magna Grecia is highlighted.

It is thus illustrated that culture is not only the artworks and the antiquities but also the relations and behaviours between people, then and now.

My warmest thanks are addressed to the Director General of the Museums of Italy Massimo Osanna, the Director of the Museum of Matera, Annamaria Mauro, and to all the contributors from Italy and the Acropolis Museum who have contributed to this exceptional attempt.

Table of Contents

INTRODUCTION
Alessandro De Pedys — 7

ESSAYS
Nikolaos Chr. Stampolidis
Remarks on the unknown Beauty of the civilisation of Basilicata — 9

Annamaria Mauro
The Exhibition — 13

Massimo Osanna
Greek Migrations and Contacts of Peoples and Cultures on the Ionian Coast of Basilicata between the 8th and 7th century BC — 17

Angelo Bottini
Indigenous Peoples and Greeks in the Ionian Arc and its Interior — 29

CATALOGUE OF THE EXHIBITS ON DISPLAY
Descriptions by Addolorata Preite, in collaboration with Carmelo Colelli, Vincenzo Cracolici and Laura D'Esposito — 47

GLOSSARY — 129

BIBLIOGRAPHY — 131

Introduction

The ambitious project *Il racconto della bellezza (The Telling of Beauty)* seals the cooperation between the Ministry of Culture and the Ministry of Foreign Affairs and International Cooperation in promoting and valorising Italy's material and immaterial heritage abroad, through an articulated programme that exhibits important centres of artefacts held in storage in Italian Institutes of Culture all over the world.
Returning to the warehouses of Italian museums means retracing the history of that enormous unexhibited heritage that makes up a museum 'inside' the museum, a primary source for study and research which also tells the tale once again of the complexity of Italian museography and collectionism. And it also means using new tools to rethink the theme of how to access said heritage.
After the initial circulation (which is still ongoing) which brought the invaluable pre-Roman testimonies of Canosa di Puglia to the Italian Institutes of Culture in Santiago del Cile, Buenos Aires, San Paolo and Mexico City, and following the exhibition of the monumental *Presepe del Re* of the Museum of Civilisation in Rome to the Institutes of Prague and Madrid in 2022 and 2023, resulting in huge attendance success, *Ancient Civilisations of Basilicata – Treasures emerging to light* exhibition marks the next chapter of this project.
The exhibition retraces the history of a territory, that of ancient Basilicata, in its material testimonies dating back to before the arrival of the Greeks, and therefore the culture of the Oenotrians, the ancient Italic people who inhabited the southern part of the region between the 9th and 6th centuries BC. The objects selected for display – first amongst them the admirable grave goods with necklaces in bronze and amber – refer to the funeral contexts of the main Oenotrian centres and make up a primary tool in understanding the social life and geography of the trades of those peoples, both before and during colonisation.
The exhibition starts its journey from the Italian Institute of Culture in Hamburg in November 2023, to then move on to Warsaw, Budapest, and finally Athens in autumn 2024.
Within this perspective, the network of Institutes becomes an exclusive stage to bring an enormous heritage - largely not displayed in museums or places of culture – finally in front of an international audience.
Celebrating the cultural heritage of the state museum network of Basilicata – including the National Museum of Matera and the museums and places of culture of the Regional Management of the Basilicata National Museums – in the very heart of Europe is a choice that strengthens cultural awareness and knowledge, and opens it up to new onlookers who are encouraged to learn more about specific territorial and cultural contexts and therefore pique, also qualitatively, the interest of the international audience.
In this initiative, with *Il racconto della bellezza (The Telling of Beauty)* the network of Institutes reaches one of the goals of its mission: it represents the privileged place where Italian culture and its main local cultural players meet with the international audience, once more defining itself a virtuous tool of cultural diplomacy.

Alessandro De Pedys
General Manager
General Management for Public and Cultural Diplomacy MAECI

Remarks on the unknown Beauty of the civilisation of Basilicata

Nikolaos Chr. Stampolidis
Director General of the Acropolis Museum

Over the centuries, millions of people have travelled across the waves and currents of the Mediterranean sea which is embraced by three continents, dubbed the "Great Green" by the Egyptians and described as "wine-dark sea" (οἴνωψ πόντος) by Homer. At times alone, at times just few, most times in large groups, people driven by great forces such as Necessity, the allure of the unknown, the connection with the land across and sometimes all of these together. Some carrying their gods and others relying on the strength of their body and weapons; some turning their eyes towards a vision of a better life and others driven by profit; yet all of them full of hope, encountering each other in coasts and on islands, both large and small, bringing with them –apart from their earthly possessions – their habits, beliefs and ideas, thereby creating a amalgam of cultural interactions, an amalgam of unparalleled cultural value.

Daring to trace and describe a world that acts and pulsates, a perpetual movement of life, fluid and ever-changing –even nowadays – with all the possibilities provided by the media and the information society, may seem – although it actually isn't – utopian. And it seems even more utopian and unobtainable, if we also add to the amalgam of the multicultural Mediterranean space the parameter of time; a time distant, a time long passed. And only people's innate tendency to discover and learn ("due to an innate love of knowledge" -του ειδέναι ορέγεσθαι φύσει- according to Aristotle), and their desire to transmit knowledge to others, can render the utopia real, convert hardship to something easy, give motivation to the journey being undertaken. Because the creation of an exhibition that aims to highlight the relationships and interactions between the peoples of a region, such as the Mediterranean, is in fact a complex journey, in which the parameters of space, time and humankind intersect. It is similar to the journey of the silver Krater of Sidon described by Homer in the penultimate canto of the *Iliad* (XXIII 40 *et seq.*, 748 *et seq.* and 778 *et seq.*), with its long and time consuming pilgrimage from its native city on the coast of Syro-Palestine, across the islands and cities of the northeast Aegean and northwest Asia Minor, possibly landing on the island of Ithaca, in the Ionian Sea.

In this large basin, formed by different seas and surrounded by coasts, archaeologists often attempt to define the journeys and routes of people from past eras, dividing the body of the earth in space and time. And they try to discern relationships and behaviours of past times through the material remains of people who lived and acted in a region, and strive to understand meanings and reach conclusions useful in the present.

A similar journey is described in this exhibition entitled *Ancient Civilisations of Basilicata – Treasures emerging to light*, which we have the pleasure of hosting in the Temporary Exhibition Hall at the Acropolis Museum. It is the fruit of the labour of many scholars who have dedicated years to highlighting the culture of a region in southern Italy, the area in the middle of the Gulf of Taranto, the land of Oenotria, today's Basilicata. So those who visit the Exhibition can admire the civilisation that the Greeks from the Peloponnese and the islands of ancient Greece encountered on their long journeys, undertaken to settle in the lands of Italy and Sicily, and mainly in the coastal areas known as Magna Graecia: because the Greece of Western civilisation was truly great.

Intentionally, I am not referring here to the previous "waves" of encounters with the Italic peninsula, that is, those during the Mycenaean period, as they were recounted in the great exhibition "Sea Routes … From Sidon to Huelva. Interconnections in the Mediterranean (16th – 6th c. BC.)" which was presented in Athens in 2003. This Exhibition focuses on the specific area of Basilicata, highlighting the civilisation of this region from the end of the Bronze Age (11th century BC) and the Early Iron Age, right up until the 6th century BC.

The exhibition includes the material remains deriving from burials or, more poetically, paraphrasing the words of Seferis: "from ghosts and phantoms, dry kisses and lips, with the curtain of time wide open". That is, through the burials of women and men, through the personal belongings placed with them by those relatives and friends who buried them, to accompany them on their great journey to Hades. These items reveal their beliefs and religious faith, their relationships and customs when they were alive. They are artifacts of the early civilisation in Basilicata, and, later on, artifacts-objects that the Greeks brought with them. In short, items swallowed up by the ground that covered the graves and now are the protagonists in this Exhibition.

Alongside and through these, the types of funeral customs clearly emerge: cremation and incineration – which were practiced in the huge necropolis near the city of Matera, in the area of Timmari hill – or interment in graves, practiced both inland and on the coast.

Some of the most important objects to accompany the deceased are the early-dating metal objects, not just weapons, but mostly bronze ornaments for garments and women's jewelry. This ritual ostentatious display of wealth during burial ceremonies reflected, not only the deceased's prestige, but also – even though at that moment the objects fell into disuse forever – the power and wealth of their "houses".

The women's jewelry, mostly made of bronze, can be compared with other similar jewelry from northern Greece and Macedonia, from Aigai (Vergina), and in a certain way suggest the relocation of populations, not just in groups, but also through marriage or other relationships (such as commercial ones). Of course, as demonstrated by rarer finds made of amber and other materials, this relationship does not exclude a connection with Etruria or, in the East, with areas of northern and western Asia Minor.

The presence of pottery imported from or influenced by the islands in the Ionian Sea, the Peloponnese (Corinth) or the Cyclades, particularly from Paros and Naxos, is remarkable, not so much in the first phase (11th-8th centuries BC), but more in the 8th, 7th and 6th centuries BC. During this second phase, there are groups of artifacts which stand out in different areas of Basilicata, such as Chiaramonte, an area where different groups of people seem to have converged – the four nations mentioned by Strabo – and the settlements-cities which developed in the wider area. The funerary offerings in graves from the area of Alianello, as well as later those in Metapontum, are open to multiple interpretations. Not only the ceramic artifacts, imported pottery or imitations from Corinth, the Cyclades (Paros -

Naxos), the Eastern Aegean (Rhodes), and the coast of Asia Minor, such as Miletus (see Herod., VI, 21 on the relationship between Miletus and Sybaris), that relate to the preparation and consumption of wine, or grave goods which refer to feminine activities, such as weaving can be traced to techniques mentioned in Homer's epic poems, but also metal jewelry such as Phrygian fibulae, weapons, jewelry and furniture of mixed craftsmanship in iron, bronze, silver, gold, amber and ivory.

In particular, the ceramic and metal artifacts from Incoronata and Metapontum (a large necropolis to the northwest), lavish objects of magnificent workmanship, seem to indicate consolidated relationships not only with Greek and Eastern imports, similar to those found in the Eastern Mediterranean and Crete, but also Etrurian, which have been often interpreted as exchanges between aristocratic families regardless of commercial relations. However, the fact that these objects were not found in public areas or sanctuaries, but are rather examples of display of wealth, remind the customs which are common in the Greek world and in areas corresponding to the Greek settlements on the Italic peninsula.

For the entire presentation of this Exhibition, held in the inviting space of the Temporary Exhibition Hall at the Acropolis Museum, which highlights the links between our country's culture and that of the Italian peninsula – a relationship still carrying a torch – I would like to warmly thank Professor Massimo Osanna, Director General of Museums at the Italian Ministry of Culture, Architect Annamaria Mauro, Director of the National Museums of Matera, and the entire Italian team. I would also like to extend my gratitude to the people of the Acropolis Museum: archaeologists Anna Vlachakis and Iulia Lourentzatou of the Department of Exhibitions; Dr Mariangela Ielo; the staff and the head of the Conservation Department Kostas Vasiliadis, and in general all those, whose names can be found in the dedicated pages in the Exhibition catalogue.

The Exhibition

Annamaria Mauro

This exhibition began as a continuation of research started last year by the Italian Cultural Institutes abroad, and is the result of an agreement between the Ministry of Culture's Directorate General of Museums and the Ministry of Foreign Affairs and International Cooperation's Directorate General for Public and Cultural Diplomacy. It aims to promote Italy's cultural heritage abroad, through various initiatives aimed at improving its use and promoting awareness. The exhibition recounted the culture of the populations that lived in Basilicata before the arrival of the Greeks, through archaeological artefacts and the history they document. Placing the Oenotrian people in a broader context has forced us to seek new connections and meanings, convincing us of the need to create a new exhibition that would present this material in its context, at the same time recounting its biography and providing a unique interpretation of the interactional dynamics between the Greeks and Oenotrians, who lived there since the Iron Age and knew how to embrace forms of coexistence and collaborations able to develop ceramic objects of enormous value. The exhibition *Ancient Civilisations of Basilicata – Treasures emerging to light* is a continuation of *The Treasures of Basilicata* exhibition, and the result of a new valorisation agreement between the Directorate General of Museums, the National Museums of Matera - Regional Directorate of National Museums in Basilicata, and the Directorate General of the Acropolis Museum in Athens.

The journey begins at the end of the Bronze Age, among the protohistoric communities of Materano, and continues into the Iron Age with the Choni- Oenotrians of the settlements on the Ionian coast and the inland valleys of Agri and Sinni. The extraordinary objects on display belong to the grave goods of male and, above all, female burials, which attest to the wealth and hegemonic position of high-status figures within the communities they belonged to, as well as revealing cultural contacts and trade with the trans-Adriatic, Tyrrhenian and Aegean regions. Particular attention is paid to the Oenotrians, an ancient Italic people who lived in the south of the region between the 9th and 6th centuries BC, on the Ionian coast and in the hinterland. The anthropological culture of death, represented by funerary contexts, is the primary element to understanding the social life of these people. At the same time, the beauty of the artefacts selected for the exhibition, especially the grave goods of splendid bronze and amber jewellery, reveals important cultural contacts and exchanges. The exhibition of these finds, which come from the sites of Guardia Perticara, Chiaromonte, Incoronata and San Teodoro di Pisticci, as well as from the province of Matera, is an opportunity to introduce some of the most extraordinary contexts of ancient Basilicata to an international audience.

The exhibition is a journey through Italy's cultural heritage, involving the Basilicata museum network and its "Treasures". These artefacts of the country's "invisible heritage", preserved in the warehouses of the National Museum of Siritide, the National Archaeological Museum of Metaponto, and the National Archaeological Museum "Domenico Ridola" in Matera, have been restored for the occasion and divided into different stages of the exhibition, with the aim of recounting a unique cultural reality, that of the peoples of ancient Basilicata, through contexts which, in some cases, are part of the invisible heritage safeguarded in warehouses, "brought to light" and put on display for the general public.

The restoration of the complete excavation of a female burial (Guardia Perticara, Tomb 399, 9th century BC) is particularly noteworthy, with grave goods consisting of metal objects: she is wearing a headdress, rings on her fingers and toes, fibulae, and a pendant in the form of a ram. It was in a fairly good state of conservation, although there was diffused cracking, some of which very deep, caused both by the decrease in humidity between the original environment and the places of conservation, as well as by incorrect movements and supports. Furthermore, the skeleton had fractures, disconnected bones, post-depositional deformations, compression fractures, extensive chipping, coherent and incoherent deposits, stains, and localised corrosion, probably caused by the acidity of the soil. The restoration project involved the following interventions: the micro-excavation of the surfaces and arrangement of the section of earth for exhibition purposes, with the removal of coherent and incoherent surface deposits, soil residues from the deposit, limestone/siliceous incrustations, saline efflorescence, and stains on the skeleton.

The exhibition itinerary, mainly dedicated to the Oenotrians, develops chronologically to highlight the cultural evolution.

It starts with the large and significant Timmari cremation necropolis (11th-10th century BC), which attests to the transition from the previous Proto-Villanovian culture.

The exhibition presents a wide selection of representative grave goods and finds, the most important of which are the valuable artefacts attesting to the wealth and hegemonic position of the deceased within the communities. Between the 9th and 5th centuries BC, the Oenotrians were settled in a large area between the coasts of the Tyrrhenian Sea and the hinterland of the Ionian Sea, in particular corresponding to today's Basilicata, where numerous necropoleis have been found. Following the Greek colonisation of southern Italy, the Oenotrians, with their extremely rich burials, demonstrated their close contact and heavy trading with the Etruscans – via today's Campania – and the Greeks settled on the coast, while at the same time preserving part of their culture. The result of these interactions was also unique forms of coexistence and integration. The Oenotrians stand out for the care they took in laying out the corpses of important people. In the earliest tombs, the men were buried with offensive weapons (spears, swords) and, from the 6th century BC, also types of Greek defensive armour (helmet, breastplates, shields). In female burials, rich ornaments in bronze, iron and precious materials are documented. They are complex parures, containing particularly striking bronze headdresses and ornaments, sometimes in gold and silver. Over time, the funerary dress accessories (necklaces, belts, pendants) were enriched with various kinds materials, in particular Baltic amber and ivory. The presence of sumptuous ornaments and exotic materials in female burials testifies to both the important position the woman held, and to the probability that some of them had become part of the Oenotrian community as a result of marriage agreements, which is further evidence of a strong social network. The Oenotrian heritage is unique, with some particularly iconic finds, including subgeometric pottery – locally produced, imitations, and imports from the colonial world – bronze vases of Etruscan-Tyrrhenian origin, body ornaments (earrings, armillas, bracelets, rings, necklaces), and funerary dress accessories (belts, fibulae, simple and composite pendants) made of bronze, iron, amber, ivory, and glass paste. A heritage that clearly expresses a socially and economically well-structured community, including families with prominent personages capable of interacting with the Greek colonists and Etruscans-Tyrrhenians, as well as of acquiring cultural and religious models over time. The refined objects have been placed in 21 display cases, divided as follows: general overview of the Iron Age, the world of the Oenotrians, Siris, Incoronata, and Metapontum. As in other areas, our knowledge is limited to burials and related funerary rituals: of note is a large cremation necropolis discovered in Timmari (close to the city of Matera), only comparable to a few others in the nearby Apulia. The bronze objects inside the urns makes it possible to place its use between the Late Bronze Age (12th century BC) and the subsequent Early Iron Age (9th century BC). Elsewhere, on the other hand, burial was practiced, with the body placed in a supine or foetal position, especially on the hill where the villages of Incoronata and San Teodoro are, a few kilometres from the site where the city of Metapontum would later rise. The gender is indicated by metal objects. The exhibition continues with the history of the Oenotrian people, who also practiced burial and used local pottery, with numerous imitations of Greek forms – especially regarding wine vessels – and there was also the presence of Etruscan laminated bronze vessels. Settlements like Chiaromonte also seem to have had particularly close relations with Sybaris, within the context of the embryonic territorial state created by the Achaean colony, which, according to Strabo, was composed of twenty-five *poleis* (cities) and four *ethne* (tribes). The journey ends with the theme of Greek colonisation in southern Italy, which occurred in different ways, depending on the origin of the newcomers. Most of the population on the Ionian coast of Basilicata were Greeks from the Aegean and Anatolia, but rather than replacing the Italic inhabitants, it developed into different forms of coexistence. During the 7th century BC, the Oenotrian people strengthened the existing settlements and intensified their "international" contacts with central Italy, the Balkans, and the eastern Mediterranean. The increase in wealth also favoured population growth, and therefore the settlements becomes larger and more populous. The Oenotrians' political and economic power strengthened, and their burials reflect the elitist figures' continuous desire to keep up with the exponents of the Greek aristocracies. The ostentatious display of precious goods such as amber from the Baltic, acquired thanks to a complex chain of contacts, became customary. The weapons in the male tombs attest to the adoption of elements of Greek armament, modified to make it look like that of heroic warriors-cavalrymen. Tools related to the consumption of wine and meat also start to appear, referring to the practice of ceremonial banquets. Greek vases or locally produced imitations were found increasingly more often in burials. In the 6th century BC, cultural assimilation progressed and Greek artefacts, for which there was an ever-increasing demand, became signs of social status, testifying to the progressive adaptation to the cultural models of the Greek colonies.

In conclusion, the heart of the exhibition recounts the Oenotrian culture, starting from the oldest contexts, dating between the 9th and 8th centuries BC; this is the period in which the abundance of metal testifies to the level of widespread wealth, the material transposition of which were the complex ornamental bronze objects. The cultural evolution continued throughout the 7th century, thanks to the grave goods consisting of splendid jewellery, testimony to the position and status of aristocratic people and to important contacts and cultural exchanges with the Greek colonies on the coast.

The exhibition ends with some finds which attest to the penetration of elements of the Greek culture in the 6th century BC. It therefore concludes with particularly refined objects, including the *deinos* from Incoronata, depicting the myth of Bellerophon, and the remarkable amber necklace from Chiaromonte, with a pendant in the shape of a Daedalic head, which are material documentation of this profound process of interaction with the Greek culture.

I would like thank all those who successfully collaborated to achieve this result (both Museum employees and management, and external professionals): archaeologists, restorers, managers and warehouse staff, technical staff, as well as those in the administrative and supervisory departments.

Greek Migrations and Contacts of Peoples and Cultures on the Ionian Coast of Basilicata between the 8th and 7th century BC

Massimo Osanna

Southern Italy, the Ionian coast of Basilicata. Between the 8th and 7th centuries BC, the sandy beaches marked by the mouths of once navigable rivers – the Sinni, the Agri, the Basento, and the Bradano – repeatedly saw the migration of Greek people. In this stretch of Mediterranean coast, one of the regions that was already occupied, in the last quarter of the 8th century BC, by the *Sybaris apoikiai* in Calabria, and those of Taras in Apulia, archaeology documents interesting phenomena of contact between the people who arrived from the Aegean and the Italic populations settled on the last hills bordering the sea plain[1]. From the second half of the 8th century BC, and well before the foundation of the Greek colonies of Metapontum and Siris, human groups from several areas of the diverse Greek world immediately came into contact with the local Oenotrians here, at the mouth of the rivers, which were convenient landing places in the absence of natural harbours such as that of Taranto. These were not the first Greeks in history to land on this stretch of the Ionian coast in southern Italy: in the second millennium, in the Late Bronze Age (13th century BC), "Mycenaean" sailors and craftsmen dropped anchor in the Basento river, to then settle temporarily in Termitito, forging important relationships with the Oenotrian people, as evidenced by the excavation of a large hut filled with artefacts, including both imported and locally made Mycenaean pottery[2].

Of the great Oenotrian settlements documented on the hills overlooking the coastal plain, the most noteworthy are the places known today as

---

[1] The classic reference book for the Greek colonisation of the West is Dunbabin 1948. However, since this book was written, over 75 years ago, the number of reference books for the phenomena of mobility and migration in the ancient Mediterranean has grown tremendously. Please at least refer to Horden, Purcell 2000; Lyons, Papadopoulos 2002; Lomas 2004; Osborne, Cunliffe 2005; Greco 2005; Hodos 2006; Malkin 2009; Lane Fox 2010; Kapp, Van Dommelen 2011; Malkin 2011; Greco, Lombardo 2012; Yntema 2013; Lemos, Katsonas 2020. Abulafia 2013 offers a recent historical synthesis of the Mediterranean from ancient to contemporary times. Osanna 2024 is the most recent reference for the region discussed here between the 8th and 7th centuries BC.

[2] On contacts between the Mycenaean world and southern Italy: Bettelli 2002. On Termitito in particular: Bianco, De Siena 1982; De Siena 1986.

Incoronata, situated in the immediate hinterland of the area where Metapontum would rise in the last quarter of the 7th century BC, and Santa Maria di Anglona, which is not far from the stretch of coast where Siris would be founded, close to today's town of Policoro.

The example of Incoronata is certainly symbolic for understanding the contact phenomena triggered by the Greek people's mobility in this area. The ancient settlement is located on a low hill near the right bank of the Basento river, about 5 km west of Metapontum. Thanks to the systematic excavations started by the University of Milan in 1971 and resumed by Rennes 2 University in 2000, we know that, between the late 9th and 8th centuries BC, this hill was home to one of the various settlements in this region, which was, according to sources, inhabited by a segment of Oenotrian people who bore the name *Chones*[3]. The high cultural standard of this community is clearly evident from the rich grave goods of the excavated necropoleis[4].

During the 8th century BC, late geometric objects demonstrate the systematic initiation of contact with the Greeks, which can be contextualised in the larger movement of Euboean peoples throughout the entire central-western Mediterranean[5]. From the beginning of the 7th century BC, however, we can perceive a substantial transformation of the settlement area: the Early Iron Age necropoleis were full, while life was mostly concentrated on the north-eastern plateau, where a significant nucleus of a settlement had already developed, of which mostly 'ditches' remain, attributed to semi-dug huts or artisanal workshops dedicated to the onsite production of pottery. New structures covered the plateau, with a rectangular plan of 10-12 square metres, a stone base and rough brick walls, filled with traditional Greek pottery, including extraordinary objects with figured decoration and artisan installations. At the same time, on the adjacent hill of the so-called "indigenous" Incoronata, where in the 8th century BC there was the nucleus of a settlement, the continuity of frequentation is evidenced by the funerary documentation: in a small strip of necropolis from the first half of the 7th century BC, there is a cluster of "mixed" rite tombs, close to that of the cremation necropoleis of Policoro: burials in Greek vessels mixed with burials in the foetal position[6].

We learn something extraordinary from the discovery of a production of Greek-type pottery, undoubtedly started onsite by Greek artisans who moved here, found alongside the sets of matt-painted pottery, the traditional Italic ceramics[7]. Various categories of painted ceramics have been found, including figured pottery, which eclectically reproduce a decorative syntax composed of geometric motifs and figurative scenes, one of the most interesting

---

[3] Out of the large number of books on the excavations carried out by the University of Milan, please at least refer to ORLANDINI 1983; Stea 1999 with previous bibliography. Regarding the excavations carried out by Rennes 2 University: DENTI 2009, 2014, 2016, 2017, 2018. Important considerations on Incoronata in the Early Iron Age can be found in COSSALTER, DE FAVERI 2008.

[4] On Early Iron Age necropolis: CHIARTANO 1994. On the Italic peoples in general, TORELLI 1988 is always enlightening.

[5] On Euboean colonization: BATS, D'AGOSTINO 1998; for Calabria: MERCURI 2004. In general, on the role of the Euboeans in the mobility in the Mediterranean during the 8th century BC, LANE FOX 2010; BRACCESI 2010.

[6] On the excavations carried out by the Superintendence of Basilicata in the Iron Age contexts of the Metapontum area: DE SIENA 1986a; 1990; 1996; DE SIENA, GIARDINO 1999.

[7] On this category of material: YNTEMA 1990.

Fig. 1. Pisticci (MT), Incoronata. *Dìnos* depicting counterposed horses.

Fig. 2. Pisticci (MT), Incoronata. *Dìnos* depicting Bellerophon fighting the Chimera.

productions of the Greek Orientalizing Period[8]. Of the numerous ceramics, the figured *dinoi*, most likely wine vessels, are particularly noteworthy. This unusual production characterised the entire region between the Metapontum Plain and Siritide, and the decoration consisted of a typical "sail" motif on each side of the imitation ring handles, and a figurative panel with counterposed horses (Cat. 32.2, Fig. 1). While the decorative syntax of these vessels – and of many other figured objects – seems to derive from the iconography of Cycladic pottery, there were many

---

[8] For a document summary of this important category of materials, see the editions on excavations by ORLANDINI *et al* 1992; ORLANDINI *et al* 1995; CAVAGNERA 1995. A first reflection in DENTI 2012. A monographic study edited by DENTI 2024 is now finally available. On Greek pottery from the Orientalizing Period: COULIE 2013. For an updated debate on the Greek world in the 7th century BC: CHARALAMBIDOU, MORGAN 2017.

other influences and models present in Incoronata: from Prototattic pottery, which appears to have inspired a beautiful *dìnos* depicting Bellerophon fighting the Chimera (Cat. 32.1, Fig. 2), to Corinthian productions, for example the elegant globular vases with linear decoration, and eastern Greek pottery, represented by, among other things, the eclectic decoration on a beautiful piece with stylised plant elements and a metopal panel depicting a hunter (Cat. 32.4, Fig. 3).

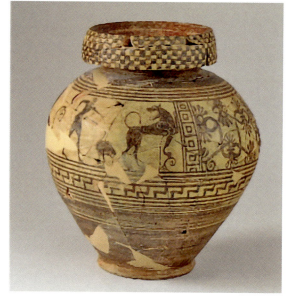

Fig. 3. Pisticci (MT), Incoronata. Globular vases depicting a hunter.

Another interesting category of materials is represented by the large kraters, or *stàmnoi*, with subgeometric patterns, influenced by the Argive-Syracusan kraters of the so-called Fusco production. Among the tableware, there are Bucchero drinking vessels (cups and *kàntharoi*), the technique of which is possibly of north Ionian origin.

Alongside the tableware, there are some truly impressive luxury products, such as the large *perirrhantèria* (ritual water basins) with relief decoration, the local production of which is also proven by the discovery of a mould fragment. In particular, there is a truly monumental piece that documents the presence of a craftsmanship tradition that until now has been largely underestimated, the Laconian one, established in the homeland thanks to regular contact with cultures other than those of eastern Greece and Crete, and, of course, with the Corinth[9]. It has been discovered among the materials found in one of the identified spoilheaps (so-called Oikos G), dated to the third quarter of the 7th century BC[10]. Figured friezes on overlapping bands wrap around the basin's cylindrical stand, recounting Greek myths and presenting the rich bestiary typical of a century marked by the influence of Eastern cultures. On the lower band there is a famous myth linked to the Labours of Heracles, the hero fighting the centaurs, depicted here as he is killing one of them; then there are two figures wrestling (perhaps Peleus and Atalanta), a hero wielding a sword and a woman carrying a vase, perhaps Menelaus and Helen, or Odysseus and Circe, and two running Gorgons. On the band above there is a battle scene depicted on the body of a fallen warrior, repeated six times, and on the upper band a divine couple, perhaps Zeus and Hera, on a chariot pulled by winged horses, repeated eight times. Finally, there are alternating lions and panthers on the rim of the basin, with an inverted lotus flower in the centre, surmounted by a scrolled palmette (fig. 4).

The precious basin designed to contain water for washing before a banquet or rituals, is a sort of encyclopaedia of archaic myth, composed for the delight of local elites, who manifested the prestige and pride of belonging to a world of heroes through this luxurious object and the mythical themes depicted (fig. 5). The myths refer to a world in which exoticism (lions, panthers,

---

[9] ORLANDINI 1980; 2000.
[10] For a broad look at Laconian culture in the Mediterranean area, see COUDIN 2009.

Fig. 4. Pisticci (MT), Incoronata. Perirrhanterion (photo by the A.).

Fig. 5. Pisticci (MT), Incoronata. Detail of the decoration of Perirrhanterion. Photo by Vincenzo Cracolici.

gorgons) was for the Mediterranean aristocracies (to which the users of such an important piece undoubtedly belonged): travel adventures and mobility by sea (the stories of Odysseus), the right marriages based on the divine model of Zeus and Hera, and the arete female warrior, are all founding values of a society with maritime connectivity.

In terms of its production, we are certain that the basin was produced onsite, as also documented by the discovery of a mould used to the reproduce one of the figurative scenes. As far as the underlying artisanal tradition is concerned, thanks to a careful comparison between the frieze depicting a battle scene and a similar scene on a krater from Sparta, dating back to the last quarter of the 7th century BC and attributed to a Laconian artisan workshop, I have no doubt that our *perirrhantèrion* is also the work of an artisan trained in the Spartan cultural *milieu*, where the evident Corinthian influence is mixed with Cretan elements[11].

The onsite production of this prestigious category of banquet vessels, intended for convivial rituals, reveals another aspect of the so-called Greek "Orientalizing" period, that is, the establishment of workshops with an "eclectic" style, started by artisans who arrived in this Oenotrian community from various parts of the Greek world, and in particular from the Cyclades, and whose artisanal skills led to "hybrid" pottery: we are in a middle region, where each of the various Greek traditions, primarily Cycladic, followed by those of Corinthia, Attica, and eastern Greece, were disassembled to create new, "international" products, because the society inhabiting these intertwining lands, as these areas on the Ionian coast have been defined, where Greeks and Italics found a new *modus vivendi* together, couldn't be anything but international[12].

It is therefore not unlikely that along with artisans coming directly from the Aegean to Incoronata in search of fortune, there were also those from new,

---

[11] Christou 1964, pp. 260-261.
[12] Giangiulio 2021, p. 31.

already structured *poleis* such as Taranto. Moreover, the latter corresponds to the closest Greek district, and its artisans may have quickly inserted themselves into a larger environment offering a variety of productions and trading possibilities, above all the Metaponto Plain (as demonstrated by, among other things, the oldest productions found in the urban temples in Metapontum, starting from the beginning of the 7th century BC).

After the first contacts made at the beginning of the 8th century, thanks to the dynamism of the Euboean people, and once the cities of Taranto and Sybaris were settled and structured, alongside the migration of people from the Aegean a *colonial* diaspora started to form, individuals or small groups of Greeks who moved to the Oenotrian settlements temporarily, resulting in the creation of "mixed" communities.

Fig. 6. Policoro (MT) necropolis in Madonnelle. Amphora from tomb 115.

Another important context on this stretch of Ionian coast, linked to the Greek migrations in the 8th-7th centuries BC, is the one documented in Policoro[13]: according to ancient writers (Strabo in particular), a Greek colony with a unique history established itself in the area around the settlement, on the Sinni river (the ancient Siris), the colonists of which coincided with an entire community that had emigrated en masse from western Asia Minor (today's Turkey, inland of Smyrna), from the city of Colophon, following the invasion of the Lydians, led by King Gyges[14]. Sources make it possible to place this event before the mid-7th century BC. However, it is more complicated than the vulgate (of which there are also several variations) embedded in the historical memory of the ancients.

The presence of Greeks in the area dominated by a hill very close to the sea, not far from the Agri river, is undeniable, thanks to the discovery of two extensive necropolis areas (on the Schirone property and in the village of Madonnelle)[15]. They are mostly cremation tombs, designed to hold the ashes of the deceased burned on funeral pyres, a custom attested more in

---

[13] From OSANNA 2024, pp. 169-217 with bibliography.
[14] LOMBARDO 1986; 1999.
[15] In the necropolis of Madonnelle, situated immediately west of the long hill dominated by the Castello del Barone Berlingeri, ca. 450 burials have been excavated; in that of Schirone, 600 metres south-east from the first, 138 burials: BERLINGÒ 1993; 2005; 2016; 2017.

Greece than in southern Italy. Therefore, alongside a few burial tombs, the necropolis essentially contains the ashes of adults, as well as the *enchytrismoi* of infants inside imported Greek vessels: not only were the vessels imported, but also the funerary customs, which are substantially different from the funerary rituals on the Ionian coast of Basilicata in the Early Iron Age[16]. In the 8th century necropoleis of Pisticci-S. Teodoro, and those of Tursi-Valle Sorigliano, the deceased was in fact buried and the corpse placed in a foetal position[17]. If we take a close look at the urns, we can recognise amphorae from Corinth, Athens (Cat. 26, Fig. 6, or similar type: Cat. 24, Fig. 7) and the eastern Aegean settlements, as well as large vessels of Greek matrix such as *pithoi, stamnoi* or *hydriai,* the production of which is documented in the coastal area of western Turkey (Miletus, for example), on the island of Euboea, and in the Cyclades (Cat. 27, Fig. 8). Alongside these Greek vessels, which arrived here as containers for food products, from oil to wine, to then be reused as cinerary urns, there are few local vessels, such as clay *situlae,* and, at least in one case, a large biconical *olla* with the typical Oenotrian matt-painted decoration. The grave goods, if present, are extremely simple (unlike the local funerary custom): *aryballoi* and *alabastra*, drinking vessels and wine cups. The reference to the banquet, the most convivial gathering in those ancient societies (and not only) is not surprising: the consumption of wine not only strengthened the group, but also distinguished the privileged people who drank it. These grave goods are all Greek: Corinthian and Eastern Greek pottery, as well as the ubiquitous Euboean imports, alongside products made locally by Greek artisans, such as the so-called Corinthian-inspired *'a filetti'* cups[18].

In one of the two sections of funerary space, there are some burials of people in a foetal position among the cremation burials, without grave goods, which refer to the funerary ritual documented in the Panhellenic tombs in the immediate hinterland of the Ionian coast, in the Bradano valley and the neighbouring Apulian area, as well as some supine burials, a position that was very popular in the innermost part of the hinterland, along the middle valleys of Agri and Sinni[19]. These are not the only "indigenous" burials documented in Policoro. Others, both isolated and in small clusters, have been identified both in the western section of the hill of the Castello del Barone (two of which are in close proximity to some 'ditches', which would indicate the presence of houses), and on the plateau that extends southwards, where today's town stands[20]. These tombs, dating between the late 8th and 7th centuries BC, containing either a small number of grave goods or none at all, are those of local people, buried near the houses, as evidenced by the discovery of a hut dating between the end of the 8th century and first half of the 7th century, situated on the southern end of the plateau, flanked by two burials with the deceased in a foetal position[21].

---

[16] On the "indigenous" world of Basilicata in general, see BOTTINI 2016A. Relatively to the southern gravitating region in the hinterland of the colonies of Sybaris and Metapontum: BOTTINI 2016B.
[17] On funerary rituals in vogue in the Greek world between the Early Iron Age and the Archaic Period: D'AGOSTINO 1996, pp. 444 ff., with bibliography. For southern Italy before the Greeks, an overview with a bibliography in BIANCO 1999A.
[18] VULLO 2012.
[19] BOTTINI 1997.
[20] Recent overview in GIARDINO 2010. For a discussion on the entire data summary: OSANNA 2024, pp. 169-189.
[21] BIANCO 2012B; BIANCO, GIARDINO 2010.

Fig. 7. Policoro (MT) necropolis in Madonnelle. Accessories from tomb 48.

Therefore, very few Italic burials in a place with hundreds of Greek tombs. If we compare this site with the finds in the nearby Santa Maria di Anglona, a settlement situated about 12 kilometres inland from Policoro, home to an important Early Iron Age settlement, we can clearly see how different the Policoro settlement was.

Here in the hinterland, various burial areas were situated on the hills overlooking the plateau dominated by the beautiful Norman cathedral[22]. Although these clusters do not seem to go beyond the Early Iron Age, a group of 27 burials were found in the section explored immediately north of the hill, which are staggered continuously between the beginning of the 8th century and the mid/third quarter of the 7th century BC.[23] The deceased are in a foetal position, laid out inside shaft tombs surrounded by a stone circle: the late 8th/7th century BC grave goods are composed of weapons and ornaments typical of the local tradition, alongside a few precious imports, such as a silver Phrygian fibula; significantly, one of these was also found in Policoro. As well as local pottery, there are also some imported Greek objects, which provides a similar picture to that of the nearby settlement of Policoro.

Inland, not far from the Ionian coast, there are no traces of the permanent presence of Greeks: the burials are all of indigenous tradition, continuing an ancient ritual without any changes whatsoever.

This funerary ritual and traces of a similar material culture, both in the use of local objects and traditional Greek ones, makes it plausible that at least some of the deceased buried in a foetal position in Policoro may have come from this community, as well as from nearby settlements located further inland, where the ritual of supine burial is documented (such as in Chiaromonte, for example)[24]. These movements of local people to the coast

---

[22] Frey 1991; 1998.
[23] Malnati 1984.
[24] Bottini, Costanzo, Preite 2018.

where Greek migrants arrived, created an eclectic landscape in the new community, marked by multiple expressions, evident in the ways they lived and how they expressed the relationship between the living and the dead.

This community, which appears to have formed in the second half of the 8th century BC, did not give rise to a *polis*, or even to an "indigenous" settlement — indeed, their ways of living and burial practices were nothing like those of an inland population. We are rather looking at a completely new experimentation for these districts, a mixed one, where people of Aegean origin structured a landscape that attracted – in many ways – local people settled in the hinterland both nearby and faraway, initiating forms of cultural hybridisation[25]. Yet, although it was not a *polis*, a Greek city, we are in any case looking at a community established by Greek people, based on "open" contact and mutual trading with nearby indigenous settlements. And they were tolerated precisely because the presence of new people gave rise to a profitable exchange on many levels, from the acquisition of resources and artisanal products (for example the exotic silver Phrygian fibula acquired by a high-status person in Santa Maria di Anglona thanks to contact with a Greek who had arrived on the coast), to the mutualisation of technical knowledge[26]. The communities formed by Euboean sailors and soldiers of fortune on the eastern coast of the Mediterranean between the 9th and 8th centuries BC, from Cyprus to Cilicia and Syria, were probably much the same[27].

An open community that attracted different groups, creating complex dynamics of integration and coexistence, focused more on maritime contacts than inland ones[28]. On the one hand, this seems to explain the presence of a massive number of transport vessels from various parts of the Aegean, of very diverse origin, particularly during this first occupation phase, and, on the other, the absence of conspicuous traces of trading in the inland communities, in the area where all the imports are concentrated in sites situated along the coast, as we will see. The presence of Greek wine cups in the tombs of local elites in Santa Maria di Anglona, alludes to the social aspect of drinking Greek wine in ritual exchanges of hospitality between newcomers and people living in the immediate hinterland[29].

In conclusion, following the phase of first contacts in the 8th century BC, the various 'colonial' groups settled during the 7th century BC, an era marked by the building of relationships on multiple levels; these were extremely fruitful decades, during which complex settlement dynamics were established, giving rise to dynamic artisanal productions. These "open" communities were not destined to last long: within just a few decades, and by the end of the century, they either ended or created new communities. In the case of Incoronata, the hill was abandoned, setting in motion, among other things, complex rituals for the closure of the settlement and its ceremonial, housing and production structures[30]. Thanks to the most recent excavations conducted by the University of Rennes, systematic traces of this desertion –

---

[25] In general, ANTONACCIO 2003; on the regions of Siris and Metapontum: OSANNA 2014A; 2014B; 2016A.

[26] VERGER 2014; 2016.

[27] On the phenomena of mobility and the presence of Euboean people in the eastern Mediterranean area, between Cilicia and Syria: LANE FOX 2010.

[28] As highlighted in VAN DOMMELEN 1998 with regard to Sardinia, the coastal communities were more oriented toward external and overseas contacts rather than becoming a reference point for large-scale trading with the inland.

[29] WECOWSKI 2014.

[30] DENTI 2014.

which was coeval with the foundation of the *polis* of Metapontum – have been found, revealing a pervasive and systematic abandonment process that was almost like a ritual closure. This involved artificially levelling the land and the creation of large deposits of Greek objects, which were dumped inside the so-called quadrangular *oikoi* and sealed away forever[31].

It is safe to say that the desertification of this important settlement was a consequence of the formation of the political structure of the Achaean *apoikia* of Metapontum in the last third of the century[32]. The recent edition of the tombs with prestigious grave goods in the necropolis of Crucinia, revealing glimpses of the life of "colonial" elites, provides important data on the political structure of Metapontum, a city that sources say was closely connected to Sybaris and the extremely dynamic northern area of the Peloponnese in ancient times[33]. The most important thing that the grave goods in the tombs in the Giacovelli property reveal, is the close interrelation between Metapontum and the coastal population of the eastern Mediterranean, indicating a city that was decidedly part of the Mediterranean network. Thanks to the prestigious and anomalous grave goods, it is clear that these high-status figures, undoubtedly protagonists in the dynamics that would lead Metapontum to becoming a city-state, were not only people imbued with international culture, but also and above all, that the roles of these men and women within their own community must have been fundamental for the entire city, for example that of priests and priestesses, responsible for sacrificial practices.

The exaltation of power, luxury, sacrifice, and banqueting are the predominant aspects that emerge from the decoding of the grave goods. The shapes and materials, all precious, refer in particular to the eastern Mediterranean coasts, reiterating the exceptional nature of this small group of privileged people who highlighted their status with the objects they possessed, flaunted and used (before being placed in the tomb). The objects testify to contacts and links between the West and East. The large number of objects acquired through the network of relationships woven by this group, evidence the phenomena of mobility and migration which presided over the foundation and growth of the Greek cities in Southern Italy (and beyond). The tombs in Metapontum therefore appear to belong to a powerful group that may have come from afar, as part of the chain migration to the Ionian coast of Basilicata that occurred in the 7th century BC. Relocations, changes of residence, hospitality relationships, and the exchange of gifts are all phenomena that can be deduced from the observation and study of the objects. Therefore, in Metapontum during the last quarter of the 7th century BC, a significant structural change took place within the settlement that had already been frequented for some time: following the "open" neighbourhoods, which arose due to the subsequent arrival of people from the Aegean and locals, the above-mentioned chain migration, and mobility phenomena, the settlements started to create "a different relationship with the territory, taking possession the land, alongside the establishment, compared to its more egalitarian beginnings, of a colonial aristocratic elite [...]. The occupation and extension of the controlled territory affected relations with the local populations, which undoubtedly manifested in many different ways: cases of occu-

---

[31] DENTI 2009; 2016; 2017; 2018, pp, 211-213.
[32] Important new data on the foundation of Metapontum have emerged thanks to the publication of the Giacovelli tombs: BOTTINI, GRAELLS i FABREGAT, VULLO 2020.
[33] BOTTINI, *et al* 2019. On the Achaeans of Greece and Magna Graecia in ancient times from the most recent GRECO, RIZAKIS 2019.

Fig. 8. Policoro (MT) necropolis in Madonnelle. *Hydria* from tomb 224.

pation and violent clashes were accompanied by other, more complex interactions"[34]. It is no coincidence that the emphatically perceptible indication of the changes which occurred during this period was the appearance of sacred areas: the visibility of the sacred – from the urban temple probably dedicated to Apollo, Hera and Aphrodite, to the suburban temple of Hera and the Palatine Tables – was a clear sign that a *polis* had been born.

With regard to Policoro, the second half of the 7th century also marked an important change in the settlement dynamics, albeit in substantial continuity with earlier ones. The continuity of occupation in Policoro is documented not only throughout the 7th century BC, a period in which the continuous use of the Schirone necropolis is attested, but also well beyond, up until the first half of the 5th century BC, as evidenced by – among other things – the continued use of the other necropolis, Madonnelle, although in different forms[35].

As for the signs of transformation which seem to refer to the establishment of a community with a Greek political system, we must first look at the obvious traces of the structure of sacred spaces, found in material documentation ranging from tombs to housing, which increased significantly in the second half of the 7th century BC and during the early decades of the following century. Other tangible signs of the transformation of the settlement area, which acquired an urban form, have been found along the edge of the plateau on top of the hill, where traces of a mighty rough brick were discovered, dating between the middle and second half of the 7th century BC, which seems to develop along the entire edge of the hill[36]: whether it was a boundary wall or a dividing wall, the scope of the discovery is remarkable in terms of being able to see the beginning of a new way of arranging the space, indicating a complex organisation of space achieved through the collective efforts of a community. But something that should certainly not be underestimated, as already mentioned, is the appearance of the first traces of sacred spaces, which were very distinct from those destined for daily activities: the building of temples in precise spaces in the "urban" area during the second half of the 7th century BC, probably from the middle of the century, is well documented by archaeological studies[37].

---

[34] Vannicelli 2022, p. 12.
[35] Berlingò 1986.
[36] On the phases of the 7th century found in Policoro: Adamasteanu, Dilthey 1978. The most recent reference books, with a bibliography, on the wall and the difficult chronological framing, are: Bianco, Giardino 2010, pp. 634-635.
[37] The first reflections on this phenomenon of the visibility of the sacred, in relation

In my opinion, these signs of transformation can only indicate that the community was developing into a city-state; a city with well-defined political and social structures. This is reminiscent of the literary tradition on the colonial experience of Siris-Polieion, an *apoikia* that saw the entire community of Colophon move to the West after the Lydian invasion, which took place, according to Mario Lombardo's reconstruction, in around 660 BC[38]. Sources say that King Gyges' occupation of Colophon caused the mass exodus of the entire community, a society that at that time must have already developed and structured a full-fledged city-state.

The community, which formed under the banner of 'inter-ethnic' coexistence in the second half of the 8th century BC, became a mixed settlement – or perhaps rather an "open" centre – during the first half of the 7th century BC, where a minority of local people moved to from inland settlements, attracted by the presence of Greeks who had arrived in waves during the Greek migrations. During the second half of the 7th century BC, the high ground became a fortified area, while a series of sacred buildings were built both inside the walls (temple near the castle) and outside, in the Varatizzo valley (temple of Demeter, temple of the so-called *agora*, the temple 'del Vallo').

Precisely in view of these clear signs, I feel it is pointless to look elsewhere, that is, a few kilometres away, for another city to name Siris-Polieion, as has been done, also recently[39]. At the mouth of the Sinni river, following the unravelling of intricately wound threads composed of many layers of tradition, there was a Greek *polis*[40], while in Policoro, near the Agri river, there was a mixed settlement on the 'periphery' of the *apoikia*, destined to survive well beyond the end of Siris.

The birth of the colonies of Metapontum and Siris-Polieion was the beginning of a new story, the former destined for power, flourishing until the 3rd century BC, the latter a short-lived city-state, the political end of which would come as soon as between 575 and 560 BC[41].

---

to the Policoro community's development into a city-state structure, are found in OSANNA 2012. On the cults in the motherland and colonies in general: LIPPOLIS, PARISI 2010. An important summary on the temples of Magna Grecia in TORELLI 2011.
[38] LOMBARDO 1983; 1986.
[39] GIARDINO 2010; BIANCO, GIARDINO 2012. This interpretation can also be found in GIANGIULIO 2021, pp. 31-35.
[40] OSANNA, PRANDI, SICILIANO 2008.
[41] LOMBARDO 1986; DE SIENA 1999; GIARDINO, DE SIENA 1999; LOMBARDO 1999; MELE 2013.

Indigenous Peoples and Greeks in the Ionian Arc and its Interior

Angelo Bottini

THE EARLY IRON AGE: AN OVERVIEW

As in many other countries, our knowledge is limited to burials and related funerary rituals, and therefore the discoveries made on the hill of Timmari are very important. The site is close to the city of Matera, where a vast cremation necropolis, probably only comparable to a few others in the nearby Apulia, was explored at the beginning of the twentieth century. The bronze artefacts inside the urns, found either interspersed with the ashes (Cat. 1, Fig. 1), or scattered around the necropolis area (Cat. 2, Fig. 2), allow us to date the cemetery's use to the Late Bronze Age (12th-11th century BC) and therefore also to the subsequent Early Iron Age (10th-8th century BC).

It is a very rare example, as elsewhere – both on the coast and in the hinterland – burial was practiced, mostly with the corpse in a supine position, lying at the bottom of the grave, although in the area of Matera (Cat. 4, 5) and in particular the necropoleis of San Teodoro and Incoronata, the ritual of placing the corpse in a foetal position was widespread: a distinctive long-standing tradition that in later times became a characteristic element of a few central-eastern groups.

The expansion of the settlements varies depending on the areas, most of which are inland, but the highland area where the aforementioned sites are situated appears to have been the most settled, along the course of the Basento river, a few miles from the Ionian coast and the site of the city of Metapontum.

The distinction between the various settlements is reflected in the differences between the related necropoleis, where there are several hundred tombs, the gender of which is usually obvious thanks primarily to the presence of metal artefacts, most of which are bronze; there are not, on the other hand, many vessels.

The female tombs are indicated by various grave goods, and in particular those found in Tomb 581 (Cat. 12), which also contained a gold bracteate disc with relief decoration.

The latter is an extremely valuable version of an object that was usually made of bronze, mounted and perhaps suspended from a belt. There are three other known specimens to date, which came from the same site (Tomb 1) and from the nearby Santa Maria d'Anglona-Valle Sorigliano (Tombs 28 and 52). This would seem to confirm that they were produced locally, by artisans who were also capable of working with raw material obtained through the wide-spread contacts maintained by the "leaders" of these communities, who would have certainly exercised meticulous control: a *modus operandi* that is inferred in the famous legend of Hieron II having doubts about the gold crown he had commissioned to be made, later dispelled by Archimedes (Vitruvius IX, 9-12).

Fig. 1. Matera, Timmari, San Francesco. Tomb 220. Cinerary urn with grave goods (pin).

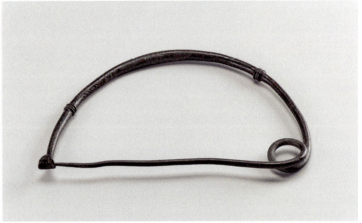

Fig. 2. Matera. Area of the Timmari cremation necropolis. Large fibula.

Fig. 3. Pisticci (MT), San Teodoro. Tomb 562. Grave goods.

As would be the case for a long time among all the peoples on the Peninsula (unlike what occurred in Greece, where wealth was put aside in temples or put to good use), the most likely ostentatious display of wealth during funeral ceremonies, of which naturally no trace has been preserved, was then followed by it being concealed and therefore destroyed. This was extravagant as much it was fundamental for confirming the status of the "family" (whatever its size and composition), as well as for strengthening its position after the loss of a member who had had a significant function, or who would have had if they had lived longer, as documented by the deposition of objects with children and adolescents.

In the male tombs, the high status of the deceased is mostly indicated by offensive weapons: one example of this is the set of grave goods 562, again from San Teodoro (Cat. 9, Fig. 3), datable to later than 850 BC, which is composed of an Italic iron "grip-tongue" sword with inserts and a bronze sheath, and the spear head of a long weapon made of bronze, an alloy (obtained thanks to the availability of metal from nearby Calabria) which seems to have made up most of their non-perishable assets.

Movement of goods and the adoption of customs

This acquired more specific characteristics during the 7th century, in parallel with the emergence of groups with the same primarily demographic growth, but which differed in many ways: in the nature and size of their settlements, although all were formed by groups linked by extended kinship ties; in the type of matt-painted pottery traditionally decorated with geometric patterns; and, as mentioned previously, in their funerary rituals, which involved either supine or flexed burial. As far as relations were concerned, they all had contact with the Etruscans, at least in part via Campania, based on relationships of a social nature rather than "mercantile" logics, and therefore also with the Greeks settled on the Ionian coasts, where specific forms of coexistence/integration began developing alongside the production of high-quality pottery, but which never extended inland.

We can see the results of this in the growing diffusion of bronze vessels, especially laminated ones and in particular the basins produced on a large scale by Tyrrhenian artisans, and, on the other hand, ceramic tableware, mainly cups, which coincided with the arrival of wines that were different from the local ones, and preluded the adoption of the tools needed to prepare them for consumption during banquets, according to Greek customs: as mentioned in a famous passage of the *Iliad* (XI, 624-641), the wine had to be diluted with a lot of water, flavoured with grated cheese (among other things...), then filtered and served.

Men at arms

As far as men of high social status were concerned, within this overall picture we see the modification of the traditional weaponry which did not provide protection for the body, except perhaps leather bodices and wooden shields – possible thanks to the acquisition of pieces of bronze plate armour, particularly helmets and greaves of the Hoplites, the citizen-soldiers of the nascent Hellenistic armies.

We must of course bear in mind that this does not indicate that these groups started adopting the forms of social and political organisation typical of the Greek *poleis*, nor consequently the adoption of the corresponding infantry tactic of a tightly packed, orderly formation. On the contrary, a small number of armed men would ride a horse, as individuals, with an order of battle that made it impossible to distinguish either status or age. The most signif-

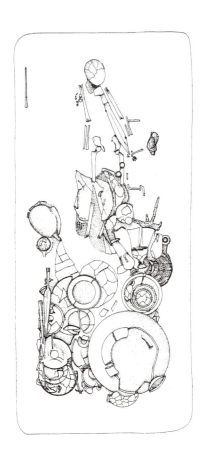

Fig. 4. Chiaromonte (PZ), Sotto la Croce. Tomb 110. Planimetry.

icant example is the grave goods of a tomb discovered at the site of Chiaromonte, composed of various distinct settlements, frequented during the Early Iron Age and up until the 3rd century BC, and in particular during the time of the Oenotrians, when, between the end of the 7th century and beginning of the 5th century, no more than four or five generations lived there[1].

Tomb 110 (Cat. 16 Figs. 4, 5), closed around 600 BC or shortly thereafter, belongs to the very extensive necropolis of Sotto la Croce, in turn divided into several differently-structured clusters. The presence of an iron horse bit and bronze harness rings indicates that it belongs to a cavalryman, heavily armoured and well-equipped like the warrior depicted in the well-known bronze statuette, from not much later, found in nearby Armento and now at the British Museum (its provenance is often said to be the Roman city of *Grumentum*, but this is unfounded).

With regard to the offensive weapons, all of which are made of iron, instead of the more common double-edged sword, the main weapon (not surprisingly laid on the chest) is a large *machaira*, suitable for striking from above (16.13). This is flanked by two long weapons placed along the edge of the grave, of different sizes and types: a spear with a spear head and butt-spike, about 2 metres long, and a slightly shorter javelin, with just the spear head (16.14-16). The same combination can be seen on a Corinthian *alabastron* reproduced in A. Snodgrass[2].

The defensive panoply, made of bronze plates, includes a "Corinthian" helmet (16.9) and a pair of greaves (16.11,12), along with the exceptional pres-

---

[1] BOTTINI, COSTANZO, PREITE 2018.
[2] SNODGRASS 1964, fig. 33.

Fig. 5. Chiaromonte (PZ), Sotto la Croce. Tomb 110. Grave goods.

ence of a pair of right arm defences (16.10); the question of whether these are imports from a settlement in the homeland, or the products of colonial workshops, is still unresolved; on the other hand, a more recent analysis of the very few examples of "Hoplite" shields, found in various indigenous settlements, demonstrates a disconcerting variety of origins.

Six characteristic Ω type hooks suggest that there was a specimen, completely disintegrated, which was not covered in metal plates.

Finally, there was a large *triton* shell with a blowhole, which probably served as a signal horn.

The importance of this man is also confirmed by the rest of the metal grave goods, composed of four objects: an *olpe*, perhaps colonial (16.5); a *phiale* (16.8); a *kotyle* (16.6); and a basin (transformed into a tripod with the addition of iron legs: 16.7), most likely Etruscan.

In terms of the ceramics, which are mostly made up of Oenotrian matt-painted pottery, the presence of an *oinochoe* (16.1) and two Corinthian *kotylai* is important because, on the one hand, they confirm the dating, which – as said – is no later than the early 6th century, and, on the other, they reinforce the reference to the consumption of wine, which can be traced back to the practice of commensality and a meat-based diet, to which the presence of iron spits and andirons refers.

Finally, there is an unprecedented object, a large lenticular flask with the characteristic pattern of concentric bands alternated with radial lines and "beads", definitely Tarquinian (Cat. 16.4, Fig. 6), dating to approximately the third quarter of the 8th century. Judging by the state of preservation, it is a very valuable object, for which we can provide two hypotheses: that it was acquired in the past and kept in the family for a long time (ancient relations with the Tyrrhenian area is certain), or (but less likely) "donated" to the deceased by an Etruscan counterpart as part of a ceremonial exchange.

Oenotria, and Chiaromonte in particular, was a point of convergence for relationships and the acquisition of customs from different counterparts, especially for men, and at least part of it – according to a widely shared opinion – was incorporated into the embryonic territorial state created by

Fig. 6. Chiaromonte (PZ), Sotto la Croce. Tomb 110. Flask.

Sybaris, made up of, as summarised by Strabo (VI, 1, 13 = C 263), twenty-five *poleis* and four *ethne*, which, at least in terms of the origin of the inhabitants, was multi-ethnic. Perhaps it was one of the *synmachoi* mentioned in the famous, yet much discussed treaty found in Olympia[3].

As we will see, this is a completely different situation to that of Metapontum in its earliest phase, as can be seen from the tombs of the necropolis of Crucinia.

Women in Oenotria

Along the various inland river valleys, the flourishing Oenotrian communities had a peculiar characteristic that distinguished them from others

---

[3] Giangiulio 2021, pp. 54-58.

nearby: the remarkable attention given to the grave goods deposited with women of high status, in which elements of traditional clothing, probably ceremonial (one naturally thinks of a wedding dress), were added to the precious products of wide-spread relations.

The excavation of burials dating back as far as the Early Iron Age, has in fact frequently brought to light the remains of the garments (dresses, cloaks...) wrapped around the corpses, arranged with great *pietas* in a supine position at the bottom of the grave (as it was, for example, in the case of Tomb 399 at Guardia Perticara: Cat. 15, Fig. 7), and of the particular hairstyles that adorned the head and face.

Around and on the skeleton, among the disintegrated fabrics, veils and probably also leather, the non-perishable elements stand out, especially the metal ones, which gradually became more intricate and sumptuous mixed-material parures (also decorating the legs, as shown by the anklets from Tomb 223: Cat. 14.1). From a Greek perspective, these objects fall into the category of *daidala*, objects that arouse wonder, worthy of being produced by Hephaestus himself: *With them then for nine years' space I forged much cunning handiwork, brooches, and spiral arm-bands, and rosettes and necklaces...* (*Iliad* XVIII, 400-401).

It is no coincidence that their recovery involves the sampling of the entire tomb, including some of the underlying soil, followed by a meticulous "micro-excavation" in the laboratory, artefact by artefact. Of particular interest is a type of hairstyle/headdress similar to a metal helmet found in the oldest tombs: in the case of the above-mentioned Tomb 399, it consisted of several circular plates inserted into a studded net; while in others (Tomb 380 at Guardia Perticara: Cat. 17; Tomb 349 at Chiaromonte: Cat. 18, Fig. 8) they were more intricate, with the main structure consisting of superimposed rings of spiral tubules covered with a studded cap, and circular plates on the sides, all of which would certainly have been attached to a support capable of holding it together.

Finally, the most predominate object among some grave goods found in Alianello (Tomb 316: Cat. 19), is a very long tubule, the same type as above, coiled around the hair to create a very heavy headdress. It is difficult to imagine these exponents of the highest social class wearing one of these within the various Oenotrian communities, if not for events and ceremonies, forced to remain motionless, or almost, perhaps sitting on wooden "thrones" like the one found in Verucchio.

Taking a broader look, the grave goods in Tomb 514 at Guardia Perticara (Cat. 20) are a perfect example of how the earliest prevalent use of bronze is associated with that of other materials of various types and origin, in particular amber. This was widely used both as a component of more complex products (belts, for example, one of the best documented accessories, together with ivory beads), and to give shape to what are known as twisted necklaces, which, at least in some cases, are rather elements suspended from clothes or belts, in turn embellished with the insertion of small objects, such as figured Egyptian pendants made of glass paste.

These were undoubtedly women of a very particular *status*: this is clearly demonstrated by the aforementioned burial cluster at the Sotto la Croce necropolis in Chiaromonte, where, close to the three main male tombs containing elements of Hoplite defensive panoplies, there is a long row of female tombs, in no apparent order that connects them as "couples", alongside which there are even more children's tombs, something that is very unusual.

Many of the related sets of grave goods are of considerable size, but at least six of them stand out for the presence of individual objects not only of a certain value, but also unique among the vast amount of goods discovered in the necropoleis throughout the indigenous hinterland of present-day Basilicata. Alongside the grave goods in Tombs 142 and 157, charac-

Fig. 7. Guardia Perticara (PZ), San Vito. Tomb 399. Section with skeleton and ornaments.

Fig. 8. Chiaromonte (PZ), Spirito Santo. Tomb 349. Helmet headdress (front/back).

terised by silver necklaces with a large pendant, it is worth noting those of Tomb 154 (Cat. 22), apparently chronologically not far off from the male Tomb 110, in which the imposing parure, as well as the set of necklaces and chains of amber pendants, includes, among other things: a thin choker of small gold beads (22.9), a pair of silver and amber earrings (22.7) and a second pair (perhaps braid holder) composed of thick amber rings inserted into a silver spiral bar (22.8); there is a pair of very elaborate pendants made of the same metal, suspended on the end of a braided cord threaded onto the catchplate of a Phrygian fibula (22.12).

As observed, it is more likely to have come from northern Greece or the Balkan region above it, unlike the pair of smaller specimens belonging to the same category, but in bronze, found in Cremation Tomb 11 at Siris (Cat. 23), which, as confirmed by S. Verger's meticulous analysis, is of Eastern origin, although he could not, however, exclude the possibility of it being a local production based on imported fibulae[4].

In the same complex, a completely different problem is posed by the small amber protome (only 4 cm high) added as a pendant to the typical large composite necklace of Tomb 96 (Cat. 21, Fig. 9), which was closed before 550 BC: an extraordinary object and, at the same time, the oldest known figurative amber object from the entire indigenous world in Basilicata and Apulia.

The ostentatious coiffure known as the *Etagenperücke*, which also extended towards the back – thereby creating a sense of three-dimensionality that was very rare even in later times – surmounted by a tall frustoconical crown (*polos*), together with the very marked features, are, in fact, typical of Hellenistic sculpture at the height of the 7th century. Its similarity to the well-known and much-discussed small bronze *kouros* from Delphi[5], for example, seems particularly significant.

---

[4] VERGER 2014.
[5] AURIGNY 2017, figs. 6.10, 6.11.

Indigenous Peoples and Greeks in the Ionian Arc and its Interior

Fig. 9. Chiaromonte (PZ), Sotto la Croce. Tomb 96. Female protome pendant.

The hypothesis of it being a Tarentine production, proposed during a reconstruction made at the time, which involved both the ivory sphinx with a face made of amber from Asperg[6], and the "winged goddesses" from Belmonte Piceno[7], became less certain on the discovery, at the same site, of an extraordinary ivory and amber box made using the same mixed material technique, although far more complex[8].

Regardless of where it was made, which is impossible to establish due to the mobility of the carvers, the Etruscan craftsmanship aimed at a "princely" client is evident, which extended, in different, yet similar forms, to all the Italic groups[9].

In the absence of anthropometric evidence, we cannot exclude the possibility that at least some of these women, adorned with jewellery or other exotic objects of great value, not surprisingly of different types and origin, were strangers in the community where they ended their lives, arriving there, wearing with their own jewellery, as part of the widespread "marriage strategies" we can imagine were an important part of relationships between elites, in which women were both protagonists and instruments,

---

[6] Fischer 1990.
[7] Mastrocinque 1991, pp. 84-85.
[8] Weidig 2021.
[9] Montanaro 2015.

Fig. 10. Aliano-Alianello (MT), Cazzaiola. Tomb 309. Pyx on wheels with tesserae.

Fig. 11. Guardia Perticara (PZ), San Vito. Tomb 502. Grave goods.

Indigenous Peoples and Greeks in the Ionian Arc and its Interior

and at times victims (according to customs that had conditioned their lives over the centuries, well beyond antiquity).

There is no shortage of evidence of this. On the one hand, referring precisely to representatives of privileged classes, it is enough to refer to one of the most famous dynastic events in ancient Greece, initiated by Cleisthenes of Sicyon's decision to offer his daughter Agariste's hand in marriage "to the best man he could find in Hellas" (Herodotus VI, 126-130). On the other, in a context of frequent wars, Pausanias (X, 10, 6) presents with stark clarity the subject of the works by Ageladas the Argive, offered by the Tarentines at Delphi to celebrate their victory over the Messapians: bronze horses and captive women (*aichmalotoi*, or prisoners of war).

In any case, their full inclusion in the local community is proven by the analogous composition of the fictile and metal grave goods: on the one hand, the presence of wine jars (also in Tomb 154, for example) suggests that they shared, at least in part or on a symbolic level, typically masculine behaviours; theoretically, we can envisage a gradual evolution, from simple preparation, as we can see in the same episode narrated in Book XI of the *Iliad* (624-625), where a woman, *Hecamede,* a slave of very noble origins, is entrusted with the complicated preparation of the wine, to their full participation in the ceremony that followed, on an equal footing or in a subordinate position to that of the dominant male figure, according to parameters (*status*, or age) that we are at the moment unable to understand.

It is also clear that they had to do equally typical feminine activities, such as weaving, according to the widespread *warriors and weavers* model, symbolised, for example, by a series of loom weights placed, once again, in Tomb 154.

The grave goods of burial 309 in Alianello (Cat. 31, Fig. 10), dating back to later than 650 BC, included, among other things, a rare set of 28 fictile tesserae for the production of very elaborate belts or ornamental bands, worn by very different and distant groups, and a pair of pyxes with ceramic lids, not decorated, one of them with wheels (extremely rare).

We can imagine they were used to contain all the essentials: tesserae, threads, weights, whorls...

Verses 130-135 of Book IV of the *Odyssey* come to mind:

And besides these, his wife gave to Helen also beautiful gifts,—a golden distaff and a basket with wheels beneath did she give, a basket of silver, and with gold were the rims thereof gilded. This then the handmaid, Phylo, brought and placed beside her, filled with finely-spun yarn, and across it was laid the distaff laden with violet-dark wool. (translation by Samuel Butler)

From a social point of view, we can therefore see the same subdivision of domestic work observed elsewhere, obviously more or less strenuous depending on the condition of the workers. It is certainly no coincidence that the deceased woman was buried with an anthropomorphic pendant made of *faïance,* probably Egyptian.

It can also be assumed that they had control over the house, in that it was precisely a domestic community: this is perhaps the significance of the presence of a fictile vessel shaped and decorated as a building (Tomb 502, Cat. 28.9, Fig. 11) among the grave goods of at least eight ancient female burials in the only necropolis in Guardia Perticara, placed alongside local matt-painted pottery. However, some caution is required, since this is a custom with many precedents, also from very different periods and related to different cultural areas, yet absent in nearby Oenotrian settlements.

Greek figure pottery on the Incoronata hill

The exploration of the Incoronata site, previously discussed by Massimo Osanna, has brought to light a huge amount of pottery, some of which is of extremely high quality; the work of ceramists and ceramic artists who came to the West from various different settlements, although well-known for their different productions, whose works are mainly dispersed along the Ionian coast. A very recent cataloguing of all the specimens found, including fragments, allowed M. Denti to create a reconstruction of the figures of the three main artisans whose works are present at Incoronata[10].

The first (referred to as the Horse Painter) whose origins lie in Paros, is distinguished by the presence of a group of his pottery in Sicily, in Megara Hyblaea; of these objects, the exhibition includes two *dinoi*, one with horses, tripods and the tree of life (Cat. 32.2), the other depicting a scene from the myth of Bellerophon fighting the Chimera (Cat. 32.1).

Instead the second (called the Lion Painter) appears to have come from Naxos; the *stamnos* with a lion (Cat. 32.3, Fig. 12) is his work. Finally, the Griffin Painter, who was perhaps Corinthian, named so for his massive polychrome *aryballos* with animalistic and anthropomorphic decoration (Cat. 32.4).

At the origins of Metapontum: the tombs of the necropolis of Crucinia

A short distance from the Ionian coast, northwest of the ancient city of *Metapontum,* there is a very extensive necropolis spread across the lower terraces of a hill. An analysis of the horizontal stratigraphy allows us to identify various burial clusters, perhaps arranged along one of the tracks that went towards the hinterland from the settlement and, more importantly, towards the *Heraion* at the mouth of the Bradano River, famous for its ancient hexastyle known as the "Palatine Tables".

In the section closest to the city, there is a cluster of thirteen burials which seem to be by far the oldest[11], a short distance from the tomb that contained a splendid gilded-silver lamina *polos*, probably from the second half of the 6th century[12].

Tombs 566 and 610 of the cluster are of particular importance. They are both cist tombs of monumental dimensions, respectively made of local stone and limestone (not present in the Metapontum area), built very close to each other one generation apart, during the early decades of the 6th century.

They are the burials of two men who died at a relatively old age; it is therefore evident that the first lived in the second half of the previous century.

The grave goods of both mainly contain objects belonging to the category of valuable possessions, *agalmata*, and probably *ktemata* (social status), in that they were not acquired commercially. In the absence of any elements of a Hoplite defensive panoply, the iron swords stand out, more as a symbol of power than as weapons, displayed in a period when the custom of denoting virility through their deposition in tombs seems to have been practiced in many parts of the Greek world. There is also a reference to the individual consumption of wine, indicated by a "personal" service consisting of a jug and a metal cup.

In the first (566: Cat. 33, Fig. 13), next to a laminated silver *phiale* decorated with a corolla composed of 16 embossed petals (33.6), referable to the widespread and long-lasting "Achaemenid" style, there is a very rare bronze

---

[10] Denti 2024.
[11] Bottini *et al.* 2019.
[12] Guzzo 2008.

Fig. 12. Pisticci (MT), Incoronata. *Stamnos* with lion.

Fig. 13. Bernalda-Metapontum (MT), Crucinia. Tomb 566. Grave goods.

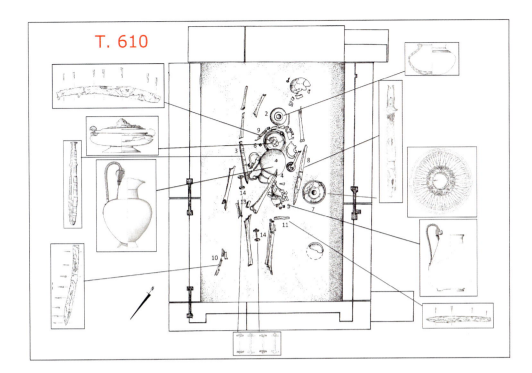

Fig. 14. Bernalda-Metapontum (MT), Crucinia. Tomb 610. Planimetry.

trefoil-mouth *oinochoe* (33.5), with a high looped handle attached with three pins, from the mouth of which emerge large heads covered in laminated silver: a peculiarity that identifies it with numerous, older Phrygian specimens. The technique used to make it, shaping a single sheet of laminated silver, also appears different and simpler than the prototypes, and confirms its attribution to a production from a different time and area, probably Miletus, as will be explained later.

Alongside this metal "pair" of objects, there is an exceptional Chiot chalice of *Middle Wild Goat Style II* (33.4): one of the oldest specimens of the very few which arrived in the West and to date the only one, together with those from Vulci, referable to the Würzburg Chalice Group.

The long (over 90 cm), type 1 iron grip-tongue sword (33.7), which was long-lasting and widespread, is equally exceptional. The hilt, decorated with ivory plates, extends into an extremely intricate mixed-material protuberance of bronze, silver and gold. The technique is clearly similar to that used in the construction of one or more types of wooden furniture (seats? a three-legged coffee table?) inspired by high-quality objects of Eastern origin, of which unfortunately there are only a few surviving fragments (33.8).

In particular, there are two forged iron pins (or two ends of the same: 33.9) with bronze and gold inserts, perhaps the only surviving part of the central axis that held together the two pairs of legs of a *diphros*, or a *sella curulis* (curule seat), such as those we see, respectively, in the weighing scene at the bottom of the laconic cup by the Arkesilas Painter, and in the paintings in the Tomb of the Augurs in Tarquinia, being carried on the back of a servant.

Then there are three bronze legs (33.10) which seem to belong to a small table or stool; a series of small bronze nails, either with a silver head partly gilded with gold, or a bone or ivory disc inserted, decorated with minute pieces of amber, could be all that remains of ceremonial furniture like Throne A in Tomb 79 at Salamis in Cyprus.

With regard to this, we can refer to the *Odyssey*, in which there is a passage referring to Penelope's chair, inlaid with ivory and silver (XIX, 55-56),

Fig. 15. Bernalda-Metapontum (MT), Crucinia. Tomb 610. Grave goods.

and, more importantly, the adjective *argyroelon*, with silver nails, an epithet of *thronos* (VII, 162; VIII, 65).

The rest of the fictile pottery is far less important in comparison: a Corinthian *alabastron* with panthers (33.1), a laconic *aryballos* (33.2), and a small grey clay vessel (33.3).

The range of objects offered in the following deposit 610 (Cat. 34, Figs. 14, 15) is far more complex. The sword (34.5) belongs to the same class, but has a wing-shaped guard, thereby confirming the later date. However, there is also a set consisting of a *machaira* and two knives (34.6-8), the first of which has a long, slightly wavy blade, and can be identified with the instrument that appears being used in scenes of the slaughter (ritual) of animals, suggesting the practice of hunting or a priestly function.

The "personal" tableware service is composed of a "Rhodian" trefoil-mouth *oinochoe* (34.3), apparently obtained by joining all the constituent parts, which are assembled, particularly with regard to the handle, using a particularly elaborate technical procedure documented by a very small number of specimens.

Close analysis shows that it is the product of a different workshop with greater skills than the colonial one to which the few vessels in the *Chiaromonte Group* have been attributed, in turn more complex than the Etruscan ones, which, on the contrary, are known to be rather numerous.

Overall, the hypothesis that the Metapontum vessel is a Greek-Eastern import, more specifically from Miletus, recognised as a production centre for "Rhodian" pottery, including the characteristic "wheel-made" *oinochoe*, seems well founded.

The wide *phiale mesomphalos* (33.4) was used as drinking vessel. It is exceptionally precious, made of laminated silver and with a gold *omphalos*, bearing a frieze composed of eight main figures of walking animals, seen in profile, alternating with fillers of varying intricacy. It is part of a very small set of specimens; at least two of them are from the ancient region of Picenum, suggesting a parallel between the *polis* on the Ionian coast and the mid-Adriatic region, again indicating the kind of display of funerary opulence that was only typical within the Panhellenic groups on the Peninsula. There are two other bronze objects among the grave goods: an *olpe* with a much less elegant shape than the previous two *oinochoai,* and a type of medium-sized "pyxes" with a screw lid, so far a unique example.

A large alabaster *alabastron* (33.2) refers to the use of unguents, as does a fictile vessel (33.1) similar to that found in Tomb 566; the shape and workmanship of a precious carved ivory comb with openwork design, decorated with the myth of Bellerophon killing the Chimera, again reflects the Eastern influence.

Overall, the Metapontum grave goods contribute to enriching the picture of the diffusion of Greek-Eastern objects both in the gravitating area on the Ionian coast and in the hinterland: it does not seem too impetuous to propose the hypothesis that they can provide archaeological verification of Herodotus' famous passage (Book VI, 21) on the relations between Sybaris and Miletus, which explicitly states that the *xenia* relationship between the two cities was superior to any other.

From an historical point of view, it finally seems indisputable that a *genos* of particular importance, already settled there in the second half of the 7th century, also contributed to the creation of the Archaean *polis,* although we don't know to what extent, one of whom – the deceased in Tomb 566 – seems to have exercised power that went beyond a mere military role, dedicated to the individual consumption of wine: it is certainly fitting with the "judicial and satrapic" undertone of a clearly Eastern matrix, both Greek and non, noted by A. Mele on an historical level. From an Hellenic perspective, it is the monocratic figure of a *tyrannos*, but in the sense of the "uncommon leadership style" suggested by G. Anderson[13].

---

[13] MELE 2013, pp. 106-107; ANDERSON 2005.

Catalogue of the exhibits on display

Descriptions by
Addolorata Preite

In collaboration with
Carmelo Colelli
Vincenzo Cracolici
Laura D'Esposito

NATIONAL MUSEUMS OF MATERA
DOMENICO RIDOLA NATIONAL ARCHAEOLOGICAL MUSEUM

1. Matera, Timmari area, San Francesco. Tomb 220 (Cf. *supra* pg. 30, fig. 1)
Late 12th-11th century BC
Cinerary urn consisting of an olla (inv. 4571.1), which contained the ashes and remains of human bones attributable to an adult individual, and a bowl (inv. 4571.2), used as a lid and placed upside down on the mouth of the olla.
A bronze garment pin is found at the base of the olla (inv. 160663), the only item in the grave goods.
The cinerary urn was protected by a stone slab (24 cm x 23 cm x 0.7 cm), placed horizontally just above the base of the inverted bowl and marked by another stone slab (stele) (80 cm x 44 cm x 14 cm), placed close to it and vertically.
Cremation necropolis, Excavation L.
Excavations: Ministry of Public Education - General Directorate for Antiquities and Fine Arts, 1901.
Bibliography: QUAGLIATI, RIDOLA 1906, pgs. 25-27, 153, 154. On the Timmari cremation necropolis see also: RIDOLA, QUAGLIATI 1900, pgs. 345-353; CIPOLLONI SAMPÒ 1999, pgs. 132-136 (with previous bibliography); NAVA 2001, pgs. 725-729, plate LX, LXI; NAVA 2002, pgs. 654-660, plates XXVII-XXIX; NAVA 2003, 132-138, figs. 5-12; MANCINELLI 2003, pages 149-152; PREITE 2017, pages 10-17; BRUNO 2018, pages 385-390, 430-432, 493-496, Appendix 4: pages 556-569, plate XXIII. Isolated or sporadic instances of cremation burials have been documented in the Matera area, specifically at Tempa Cortaglia (Accettura, MT) and Monte Croccia (Oliveto Lucano, MT). Additionally, in the Metaponto area, such findings have been recorded at Pizzica (Bernalda-Metaponto, MT). NAVA 2003, pg. 132, note 5 (with previous bibliography); in Siritide, in Tursi (MT) in the Rabatana-Castello area and in the Cozzo San Martino area (Tursi, MT): BIANCO *ET AL.* 1996, pg. 45; BIANCO 1999B, pg. 22; BIANCO 1999C, pgs. 54-56.

Cinerary urn
1. 1. Olla
Dark brown fine ware pottery. Hand-shaped vase; smoothed surfaces. Reassembled and integrated.
H 27 cm; rim: diam. 14.5 cm; body: max diam. 24 cm; base: diam. 12.5 cm; wall: thick. 0.9 cm.
Biconical body vase. Rounded rim; slightly flared lip; short, wide neck with a concave profile; rounded shoulder; flat base.

Matera, National Museums of Matera - Domenico Ridola National Archaeological Museum. Inv. 4571.1.

1. 2. Bowl
Dark brown fine ware pottery. Hand-shaped vase; smoothed surfaces. Reassembled and integrated.
H 10.5 cm; rim: diam. 17.5 cm; body: max diam. 18 cm; base: diam. 9 cm; wall: thick. 0.9 cm.
Flat rim; curved indented lip; deep bowl tapering downwards, flat base.
Matera, National Museums of Matera - Domenico Ridola National Archaeological Museum. Inv. 4571.2.

Grave goods
1. 3. Garment pin
Late 12th-11th century BC
Bronze.
Intact.
Length 12.5 cm; stem: diam. 0.3 cm; upper end (head): h 1.1 cm, diam. 0.9 cm.
Garment pin with an upper end (head) featuring a flattened biconical globe, topped by a short appendage with a quadrangular section that is bent and irregularly expanded. The stem is straight with a circular section, while the lower end (tip) is tapered and pointed.
Matera, National Museums of Matera - Domenico Ridola National Archaeological Museum. Inv. 160663.
Bibliography: QUAGLIATI, RIDOLA 1906, pg. 93, fig. 104. The garment pin belongs to the vase-head Type, Timmari type: CARANCINI 1975, pg. 245, nr. 1864; plate 56, nr. 1864.

Area of the Timmari cremation necropolis
2. 1. Large ceremonial dress fibula (Cf. *supra* pg. 30, fig. 2)
Late 12th - 11th century BC
Bronze.
Intact.
H 11.2 cm; width 17.5 cm; central arch: diam. 0.8 cm; spring: diam. 0.45 cm; pin: diam. 0.4 cm; catchplate: h 0.8 cm, width cm 1.2, thick. 0.15 cm.
Large semi-circular fibula with a simple arch; the arch is made of wire with a circular section, featuring a slightly thickened central part and two lateral nodules composed of three adjacent plastic ridges. The spring has a single coil with a circular section; the pin is straight with a circular section; the short, symmetrical catchplate has a C-shaped section.
The entire arch is engraved with intricate modular patterns, including circles, herringbone designs, and zigzags.
Sporadic discovery occurred in 1901.
Matera, National Museums of Matera - Domenico Ridola National Archaeological Museum. Inv. 170618 (4192).
Bibliography: RIDOLA 1901, pg. 36, fig. A. The fibula falls into Type 19: Large simple arch fibulae with two nodules, Timmari type: LO SCHIAVO 2010, pages 101, 102, nr. 64 (vol. 1); plate 7, no. 64 (vol. 3). Cf. MAGGIULLI 2005, pg. 312.
Similar decorative devices are known on several pieces of simple-arched bronze fibulae, with or without nodules/ribs, from funerary contexts in southern Italy (LO SCHIAVO 2010) and from the trans-Adriatic area where they are documented both on fibulae and on *torques* (BATOVIC 1980).

1.

Origin unknown
3. 1. Pair of large ceremonial fibulae (fig. 1)
9th century BC
Bronze.
Intact.
Length 31 cm; shielded arch: length 16.5 cm, width 15 cm; pin: diam. 0.3 cm; chain: length 33.5 cm.
Pair of large fibulae joined by a small chain. Shielded arch fibula. The arch consists of a lamina with a circular outline, featuring a front and rear section made of a bar with a circular section, separated from the shield by a slight ridge. The front arch is bent at a right-angle and ends in a symmetrical triangular catchplate with a low back, wide base, and semi-circular curve. The rear arch forms a large single-coiled spring and a circular section; the pin is straight with a circular section.
The shield features both plastic and engraved decoration: five thin longitudinal ribs are arranged to create an oval pattern, with a straight central rib flanked by two curved ribs on each side. In the centre there are two engraved swastikas; on the sides of the curved ribs there are elongated rhomboidal motifs created with engraved lines. The perimeter of the shield is bordered with a pattern of triangles with engraved lines (wolf's tooth motif). The fibulae are connected by a double-ring chain, of a circular shape.
Findings acquired following seizure.
Matera, National Museums of Matera - Domenico Ridola National Archaeological Museum. Inv. 23M591-2.113, 23M591-2.114.
Bibliography: the two fibulae have never been exhibited before; for comparison they fall into Type 417: Shielded arch fibulae with five ribs, Castiglione di Paludi type: Lo Schiavo 2010, pg. 819, nr. 7446 (vol. 1); plate 598, no. 7446 (vol. 3).

4. Matera, Santa Lucia al Bradano area. Tomb 1 (fig. 2)
Second half of the 9th - first half of the 8th century BC
Stone cist tomb made with stone slabs (length 1 m; width 0.50 m), inserted into and covered by a stone tumulus with a diameter of 4 m, containing the inhumation of an adult individual deposited in a foetal position.
The tomb, found on the property of Mr. Giovanni Colucci, was part of a vast stone tumulus necropolis, explored between January and September 1902 by Domenico Ridola.
Bibliography: Lo Porto 1969, pgs. 122-124; Bianco 1999a, pgs. 148, 150.

Grave goods
4. 1. Fibula
Second half of the 9th - first half of the 8th century BC
Bronze.
Reassembled. Parts missing on the catchplate.
H 6 cm; length 18 cm.
Serpentine arch fibula, featuring a circular section, an eyelet, and a single-coiled spring, also with a circular section. The pin is curved with a circular section, and the long, asymmetrical catchplate has a J-shaped section.
Herringbone decoration on both arches (front and centre).
Matera, National Museums of Matera - Domenico Ridola National Archaeological Museum. Inv. 4208.
Bibliography: Lo Porto 1969, pg. 123, fig. 1, 2, fig. 21, 2. The fibula falls into Type 341: Southern serpentine fibulae of circular section bar with herringbone decoration: Lo Schiavo 2010, pg. 669, nr. 5741 (vol. 2), plate 430, no. 5741 (vol. 3).

4. 2. Fibula
Second half of the 9th - first half of the 8th century BC
Bronze.
Intact. Deformation of the catchplate.
Length 13 cm; spiral: diam. 6.5 cm.
Double spiral fibula with figure-eight connection, originally one-piece; straight pin, circular section; deformed catchplate, made of wire, circular section. Note the broken spring, which was remedied in ancient times with a repair carried out by flattening the end of the spring and fixing it to the spiral with a small bronze nail.
Matera, National Museums of Matera - Domenico Ridola National Archaeological Museum. Inv. 4206.
Bibliography: Lo Porto 1969, pgs. 123, 124, fig. 1, 3. The fibula falls into Type 431: Spectacled fibulae with figure-eight connection, one piece: Lo Schiavo 2010, pgs. 841, 842, nr. 7665 (vol. 2), plate 629, no. 7665 (vol. 3).

4. 3. Pendant
8th century BC
Bronze.
Intact.
Length 25.5 cm; ring: diam. 5.1 cm, thick. 0.8 cm; chains: length 20.5 cm; rings: diam. 0.9-1 cm.
A large ring with a rhomboid section, to which seven chains are attached. Each chain is composed of nineteen rings, also with a rhomboid section, linked one inside the other. Two additional smaller rings, also rhomboid in section, are inserted into the final ring.
Matera, National Museums of Matera - Domenico Ridola National Archaeological Museum. Inv. 4209.
Bibliography: Lo Porto 1969, pgs. 123, 124, fig. 1, 1. Cf. with double ring chains: Chiartano 1994, pgs. 96, 97, T. 169, L (vol. I), plate 7, T. 169, L (vol. II); pg. 211, T. 351, H (vol. I), plate 83, T. 351, H (vol. II); Chiartano 1996, pg. 35, N, plate 5, N (attached to an anthropomorphic plaque) (vol. III); pg. 52, T. 515, pl. 17, I (vol. III); Bianco et al. 1996, pgs. 43, 52, 53, nr. 1.6.14; Cerzoso, Vanzetti 2014, pg. 130, description136, pg. 299, plate 11, 136 (inserted on the pin of the serpentine arch fibula, in one piece); pg. 157, description 302, pg. 311, pl. 169, 302.

5. Matera, Santa Lucia al Bradano area, tumulus necropolis.
5.1. Bracelet (fig. 3)
Late 9th - first half of the 8th century BC
Bronze.
Intact.
Length 22 cm; diam. 8 cm; ribbon: width 1.5 cm.
Bracelet made of a very thin bar, with a median rib, with nine coils. The ends, tapered, are folded into a curl.
The entire ribbon is engraved with intricate motifs of thin oblique and parallel segments, arranged in various combinations: zig-zag, herringbone, and wolf's teeth patterns.
Sporadic discovery occurred in 1902.
Matera, National Museums of Matera - Domenico Ridola National Archaeological Museum. Inv. 164899 (12102).
Bibliography: Lo Porto 1969, pgs. 128, 129, figs. 7, 8; Bianco 1999a, pg. 152, fig. 7. Cf. Chiartano 1994, pg. 103, T. 178, A (vol. I), plate 12, T. 178, A (vol. II); pg. 168, T. 186, C (vol. I), plate 16, T. 186, C (vol. II); pg. 193, T. 239, B (vol. I), plate 36, T. 239, B; pg. 120, T. 295, G (vol. I), plate 62, T. 295, G; pg. 215, T. 361, B (vol. I), plate 87, T. 361, B (vol. II); Chiartano 1996, pg. 50, T. 512, A, plate 15, T. 512, A (vol. III); Pacciarelli 1999, pg. 172, 6, plate 93, A: T. 131, 6; pg. 175, 19, plate 100, T. 145 bis, 19.

3.

6. Matera, Due Gravine area, Masseria Rizzo. Tomb 3 (fig. 4)

Late 8th - early 7th century BC

Cist tomb made with slabs and stones (h 0.50 m; length 1.30 m; width 0.65 m), inserted and covered by a tumulus of stones (d. 8 m). The cist was located in the centre of the tumulus and contained the remains of an adult individual in a foetal position on its left side with his skull facing east.

A second cist made of stone slabs, of smaller dimensions (h 0.25 m; length 0.65 m; width 0.30 m), which had already been disturbed, was located near the internal SW edge of the tumulus.

The tomb, not isolated, was part of a tumulus necropolis, explored in September 1926 by Domenico Ridola and Ugo Rellini.

Bibliography: Lo Porto 1969, pgs. 133-139, figs. 15-21; Bianco 1999a, pgs. 148-150, fig. 5.

Grave goods

6. 1. Small olla

Late 8th century BC

Matt-painted pottery. Purified pink clay. Hand-shaped vase.

Reassembled and integrated. Without a handle. Parts missing on the lip/rim. Decoration at times faded.

H 13.5 cm; rim: diam. 10 cm.

Globular body. Tapered rim; wide flared lip; truncated conical neck; rounded shoulder; flat profiled base, slightly concave; vertical ribbon-shaped handles, set from under the lip to the shoulder/body junction.

Two-tone painted decoration in black and reddish-brown. On the lip is a radial motif in black (type LR3.1, Nava *et al.* 2008); o the lip and neck, there is a wide band (2 cm) accompanied by a thinner black band. The neck features two squares outlined by double bands, which laterally define the handle areas, with a "broken line" motif inside, also defined by a double black band. On the shoulder, a large reddish-brown square is present, with a prominent black swastika at its centre. The body is adorned with a delimiting band with hanging black elements. On the handles is a motif with two lateral bands with three series of horizontal segments in black inside, spaced apart.

Matera, National Museums of Matera - Domenico Ridola National Archaeological Museum. Inv. 4525/b.

Bibliography: Lo Porto 1969, pgs. 135, 136, fig. 18, 2, fig. 19. Cf. Yntema 1990, pgs. 201, 202, fig. 184, 16; Nava *et al.* 2008, pgs. 269, 270, fig. 17, LR3.1.

6. 2. Small jug

Matt-painted pottery. Purified pink clay. Hand-shaped vase.

Reassembled and integrated. Decoration at times faded.

H (including handle) 11 cm; rim: diam. 5.5 cm.

Ovoid body. Rounded rim; wide flared lip; flat base. Vertical ribbon-shaped handle set from lip to shoulder/body junction.

Two-tone painted decoration in black and reddish-brown. On the body, alternating broad bands of black and reddish-brown. On the handle, there are two marginal bands in black and one, central, in red.

Plastic decoration: on the handle there are three small circular tablets, one on the top, two on the lower end.

Matera, National Museums of Matera - Domenico Ridola National Archaeological Museum. Inv. 4525/a.

Bibliography: Lo Porto 1969, pgs. 135, 136, fig. 18, 1.

6. 3. Fibula
Late 8th - early 7th century BC
Bronze, iron.
Not intact. Pin missing; parts missing on the catchplate.
Length 8 cm.
Fibula with a dragon-shaped arch made of bar with a rounded section and upper edge; the anterior arch has a rhomboid expansion at mid-length. The arch has two elbows: on the front one there is a pair of bars ending with two small globes; on the back one a transverse bar. The back of the fibula is made of bar, with a rectangular section, with a fold-fastener consisting of two small lateral pins expanded at the ends. Presence of iron and a small nail corresponding to the fold-fastener, probable repair due to the pin breaking. Long symmetrical J-section catchplate.
Matera, National Museums of Matera - Domenico Ridola National Archaeological Museum. Inv. 4185.
Bibliography: Lo Porto 1969, pg. 137, fig. 20, 5, fig. 21, 7. The fibula falls into Type 390: Dragon fibulae with a pair of bars and a transverse bar: Lo Schiavo 2010, pg. 781, nr. 7061 (vol. 2), plate 564, no. 7061 (vol. 3).

6. 4. Fibula
Late 8th - early 7th century BC
Bronze, iron.
Not intact. Pin removed; reassembled catchplate.
Length 9.5 cm.
Fibula with a dragon-shaped arch made of bar with a rounded section and upper edge; the anterior arch has a rhomboid expansion at mid-length. The arch has two elbows: on the front one there is a pair of bars ending with two small globes; on the back one a transverse bar. The back of the fibula is made of bar, with a rectangular section, with a fold-fastener consisting of two small lateral pins expanded at the ends. Presence of iron and a small nail corresponding to the fold-fastener, probable repair due to the pin breaking. Long symmetrical J-section catchplate.
Matera, National Museums of Matera - Domenico Ridola National Archaeological Museum. Inv. 4187.
Bibliography: Lo Porto 1969, pg. 137, fig. 20, 6. The fibula falls into Type 390: Dragon fibulae with a pair of bars and a transverse bar: Lo Schiavo 2010, pg. 781, nr. 7062 (vol. 2), plate 564, no. 7062 (vol. 3).

6. 5. Pendant
Bronze.
Not intact. Part missing on one of the expanded ends.
Length 5.8 cm; max width 2.5 cm.
Pendant composed of a trapezoidal plate with a rectangular section, featuring a widened lower end and a concave base. The upper end is ring-shaped, with an elliptical section.
Matera, National Museums of Matera - Domenico Ridola National Archaeological Museum. Inv. 4183.
Bibliography: Lo Porto 1969, pg. 137, fig. 20, 4.

6. 6. Spoke phalera
Bronze.
Intact.
Diam. 4.7 cm.
Phalera made up of three concentric rings, with a rhomboid section, joined at four points by eight small segments.

Matera, National Museums of Matera - Domenico Ridola National Archaeological Museum. Inv. 4181.
Bibliography: Lo Porto 1969, pgs. 136, 137, fig. 20, 3.

6. 7. Suspension ring
Bronze.
Intact.
Diam. 4.5 cm.
Lenticular section suspension ring.
Matera, National Museums of Matera - Domenico Ridola National Archaeological Museum. Inv. 23M591-1.5 (4180).
Bibliography: Lo Porto 1969, pgs. 136, 137, fig. 20, 1.

6. 8. Suspension ring
Bronze.
Intact.
Diam. 3 cm; bar: diam. 0.4 cm
Suspension ring with circular section.
Matera, National Museums of Matera - Domenico Ridola National Archaeological Museum. Inv. 23M591-1.3 (4184).
Bibliography: Lo Porto 1969, pgs. 136, 137, fig. 20, 2.

6. 9. Amber necklace
Amber.
Intact. With some beads missing.
Length 6.2 cm; beads: diam. from 1.2 cm to 0.5 cm.
The necklace is composed of fourteen beads in various shapes and sizes: the largest, a bulla, is placed at the centre, while the others—smaller and of quadrangular, spheroidal, and cylindrical forms—are arranged in a graduated sequence from the ends toward the centre.
Matera, National Museums of Matera - Domenico Ridola National Archaeological Museum. Inv. 4182.
Bibliography: Lo Porto 1969, pg. 137, fig. 20, 8.

7. Miglionico (prov. of Matera), Serra San Giovanni area. Tomb 1 (fig. 5)
Finds discovered by chance in an area belonging to a private individual, in the Serra San Giovanni area, already known for the presence of shaft and stone slab cist burials.
On 4 December 1924, Mr. Eustachio Cappiello, the landowner, entrusted them to Domenico Ridola, and they were subsequently incorporated into the Museum's collection.
The attribution of the finds to a single grave good (Tomb 1) is based on the association proposed by Lo Porto, which was established through comparisons with contemporary funerary contexts in the Montescaglioso area (province of Matera).
Bibliography: Lo Porto 1973, pgs. 195, 196, plate XLV.

Selected grave goods
7. 1. Fibula
Late 7th century BC
Bronze.
Reassembled and integrated (catchplate); missing half of the pin.
Length 9.8 cm; catchplate: length 5.3 cm.
Fibula with a rectangular section double-bent bar arch, from the sides of which seven small globes protrude; double-coiled spring, of circular section; straight pin, of circular section, very long symmetrical J-section catchplate. The front part of the arch shows a repair carried out in ancient times with a small bronze nail.

5.

Matera, National Museums of Matera - Domenico Ridola National Archaeological Museum. Inv. 152060 (12324).
Bibliography: Lo Porto 1973, pg. 196, nr. 5, plate XLV, 6. The fibula falls into Type 412: Elbow fibulae with globes, Montescaglioso type: Lo Schiavo 2010, pg. 809, nr. 7328 (vol. 2), plate 585, no. 7328 (vol. 3).

7. 2. Pendant in the shape of a horse
Bronze.
Intact.
H 4.2 cm; length 5.2 cm.
Pendant in the form of a stylised quadruped (horse protome). Elongated head with open mouth; eyes rendered with engraved circles and central dot; barely visible ears; cylindrical trunk; short arched tail; tapered legs. On the head there is a double protuberance, perhaps representing a bird, and on the rump, a stylised dove. On the back, fused to the body, there is a suspension hook, with an elliptical section.
Matera, National Museums of Matera - Domenico Ridola National Archaeological Museum. Inv. 152063 (12327).
Bibliography: Lo Porto 1973, pg. 196, nr. 6, plate XLV, 4. Cf. Tabone 1996, pgs. 87, 88, 98, plate I; Mazzei 2010, pg. 75, base fig., c; pg. 78, top fig., a; Bolla 2021, pgs. 84-87, cat. 82-85.

7. 3. Spearhead
Forged iron.
Not intact.
Length 29 cm; tip: max. width 4 cm, thick. 1.3 cm; handle: diam. 2.2 cm, thick. 0.4 cm.
Spearhead in foliated lamina with median rib and hollow cylindrical handle, with circular section. Horizontal mouldings on the lower end of the handle.
Matera, National Museums of Matera - Domenico Ridola National Archaeological Museum. Inv. 152339 (12330).
Bibliography: Lo Porto 1973, pg. 196, nr. 7, plate XLV, 3, 1.

8. Miglionico (prov. of Matera), Serra San Giovanni area. Tomb 2 (fig. 5)
Finds discovered by chance in an area belonging to a private individual, in the Serra San Giovanni area, already known for the presence of shaft and stone slab cist burials.
On 4 December 1924, Mr. Eustachio Cappiello, the landowner, entrusted them to Domenico Ridola, and they were subsequently incorporated into the Museum's collection.
The attribution of the finds to a single grave good (Tomb 2) is based on the association proposed by Lo Porto, which was established through comparisons with contemporary funerary contexts in the Montescaglioso area (province of Matera).
Bibliography: Lo Porto 1973, pgs. 195, 197, plate XLV.

Selected grave good
8. 1. Fibula
Late 7th - early 6th century BC
Bronze.
Not intact. Without the pin tip.
Length 6 cm; catchplate: length 2,9 cm.
Fibula with a simple arch, slightly thickened, with a rhomboidal section; double-coiled spring, with a circular section; straight pin, with a circular section; long symmetrical catchplate, with a J-shaped section with a flat

top and a raised terminal button, with a rhomboidal profile and circular section.
Matera, National Museums of Matera - Domenico Ridola National Archaeological Museum. Inv. 152061 (12325).
Bibliography: Lo Porto 1973, pg. 197, nr. 6, plate XLV, 5. The fibula falls into Type 258: Arch fibulae and catchplate with raised terminal appendage, pre-Chartreuse or pseudo-Chartreuse type: Lo Schiavo 2010, pg. 551, nr. 4844 (vol. 1), plate 337, no. 4844 (vol. 3).

National Archaeological Museum of Metaponto

9. Pisticci (prov. of Matera), San Teodoro area. Tomb 562 (Cf. *supra* pg. 30, fig. 3)

Second half of the 9th - first half of the 8th century BC
Rectangular shaft tomb (length: 2.40 m; width: 1.25 m), oriented north-south, bordered with stones and pebbles of various sizes, particularly numerous along the northern and eastern sides of the structure.
Inhumation burial of adult male individual, laid in a foetal position on his right side.
Excavations: Archaeological Superintendency of Basilicata, year 1988.
Never exhibited before.

Grave goods
9. 1. Fibula
Second half of the 9th century BC
Bronze.
Reassembled.
Length 11.3 cm.
Two-piece fibula. A serpentine arch with a trapezoidal outline, composed of a twisted bar (central arch) and rectangular section bar (front and rear arch). It features two single-coiled eyelets with a quadrangular section. The front arch terminates in two lateral pseudo-coil and a hammered spiral-disc catchplate. The rear arch is fitted into the hole of the straight pin, which has both rectangular and circular sections, and is topped with a biconical apical globe head.
There are no visible decorations on the front arch, the back arch and on the catchplate.
Bernalda-Metaponto (prov. of Matera). National Archaeological Museum of Metaponto. Inv. 314395.
Bibliography: the fibula for comparison falls into Type 323: Serpentine fibula, in two pieces, with a quadrangular-shaped arch, twisted central part of the arch, spiral-disc catchplate, pin with globular or biconical head: Lo Schiavo 2010, pg. 641, nr. 5497C (arch and pin), pgs. 640, 641, nrs. 5494, 5498B (catchplate) (vol. 2), plate 391, nr. 5497C, plates 390, 392, nrs. 5494, 5498B (vol. 3).

9. 2. Razor
9th century BC - first half of the 8th century BC
Bronze.
Some parts missing on the edges.
Length 10 cm; width 6 cm.
Razor consisting of a rectangular blade with slightly convex cuts. Handle in the shape of a bar loop, with a quadrangular section, with a central part twisted twice, with flattened ends nailed to the blade.
Bernalda-Metaponto (prov. of Matera). National Archaeological Museum of Metaponto. Inv. 314397.

Bibliography: the razor for comparison falls within the Cairano Type: Bianco Peroni 1979, pg. 38, nrs. 177, 179; plate 15, nr. 177, plate 16, nr. 179.

9. 3. Sword with scabbard
Second half of the 10th - early 9th century BC
Bronze, iron.
Parts missing on the scabbard and sword; detached tip.
Length 51 cm.
Short sword of the Italic type. Iron blade with a Grip-tongue sword-style hilt, flaring out with a rounded angle at the base and ending in a T-shape with a curved upper edge. The hilt is covered by a bivalve bronze casing with rounded shoulders and a semi-circular recess, secured with a visible bronze nail. The short blade is inserted into the scabbard.
Torre Galli type scabbard. Bronze lamina wrapped with a tip ending in a disc and appendix. Traces of decoration engraved with oblique, parallel and close-set segments are visible on the edge of the scabbard.
Bernalda-Metaponto (prov. of Matera). National Archaeological Museum of Metaponto. Inv. 314396.
Bibliography: the sword with scabbard for comparison falls into the Torre Galli Type: Bianco Peroni 1970, pgs. 79-82, plate 28, nrs. 194-196; Bianco, Tagliente 1993, plate 14; pg. 55, fig. 25; Pacciarelli 1999, pg. 327, plate 101, B: T. 147, 4; pg. 328, plate 102, T. 149, 10.

9. 4. Spearhead
Second half of the 9th - first half of the 8th century BC
Bronze.
Intact.
Length 31.1 cm; tip: max width 5.7 cm; handle: diam. 2.2 cm.
Spearhead in foliated lamina with median rib and hollow sub-cylindrical handle; two lateral holes, opposite, present in the middle of the handle.
Bernalda-Metaponto (prov. of Matera). National Archaeological Museum of Metaponto. Inv. 314392.
Bibliography: Cf. Chiartano 1994, pg. 117, T. 390, B (vol. I), pl. 59, T. 290, B (vol. II).

10. Pisticci (prov. of Matera), San Teodoro area. Site 19. Tomb 9 (fig. 6)
Second half of the 9th - first half of the 8th century BC
Rectangular shaft tomb (length 2 m; width 1.10 m) bordered with stones and pebbles of various sizes, also present in a scattered manner on the roof. Inhumation burial of an adult female, of which few remains remain, which would seem to indicate a deposition in a foetal position on the left side.
Excavations: Superintendency for Archaeological Heritage of Basilicata, year 2001. The burial was explored as part of the preventive archaeology work for the construction of the Eni Viggiano-Taranto oil pipeline.
Bibliography: Nava 2001, pg. 741; Nava 2002b, pgs. 669, 670, plate XXXIV, 2; De Siena, Preite 2016, pgs. 219, 223, fig. 26.

Grave goods
10. 1. Jug
Fine ware pottery, dark brown. Hand-shaped vase; smoothed surfaces.
Reassembled and integrated; surfaces at times eroded.
H 22 cm; rim: diam. 10 cm; body: max diam. 16.5 cm.
Expanded body tending towards biconical. Flat rim with a flared lip; a swollen neck defined by a recess; rounded shoulder; slightly concave,

profiled base; vertical handle with an elliptical section, extending from the lip, with a slight upward curve, to the upper half of the shoulder.
Plastic decoration featuring three ellipsoidal ashlars evenly spaced at the junction between the shoulder and the widest part of the body; on the upper part of the shoulder, nearly aligned with the three ashlars, there are three circular cupellas.
Bernalda-Metaponto (prov. of Matera). National Archaeological Museum of Metaponto. Inv. 324245.
Bibliography: Cf. CHIARTANO 1994, pg. 206 (vol. I), plate 48, T. 264, B1 (vol. II) with double *cupellas*; COLELLI, JACOBSEN 2013, pgs. 254-255, fig. 58, plate 115.

10. 2. Dipper Juglet
Fine ware pottery, dark brown. Hand-shaped vase; smoothed surfaces.
Intact. Small part missing on the handle; surfaces eroded in places.
H 7.1 cm; rim: diam. 8.5 cm; body: max diam. 9.8 cm; wall: thick. 0.5 cm.
Lenticular body dipper juglet. Rounded rim; slightly flared lip; rim shoulder; flat base; raised ribbon-shaped handle, rectangular in section, set from the rim to the point of junction of the shoulder/maximum expansion of the body.
Bernalda-Metaponto (prov. of Matera). National Archaeological Museum of Metaponto. Inv. 324246.

10. 3. Headband tiara
Second half of the 9th century BC
Bronze.
Studs and large ring: intact; small ring: incomplete. The tiara is recomposed.
Reassembled tiara: length 34 cm; studs: diam. 1.1 cm; small ring: diam. 1.7 cm; large ring: diam. 2.8 cm.
Headband tiara consisting of ninety-five hemispherical cap studs with internal hook, distributed in three horizontal rows, with two circular section retaining rings at the ends.
Bernalda-Metaponto (prov. of Matera). National Archaeological Museum of Metaponto. Inv. 324267 (studs), inv. 324268 (small ring), inv. 324271 (large ring).
Bibliography: BIANCO, AFFUSO, PREITE 2021, pgs. 137-139 (volume I), pgs. 489, 493, 496, 498, figs. 1-b, 5, 8, 10 (volume II).
The headband tiara, decorated with small studs applied on a support made of perishable material (fabric or leather), with or without connecting ring(s), is also documented in the Oenotrian necropoleis of the internal area of the Agri-Sauro and Sinni river valleys from the first half of the 9th to the first half of the 6th century BC. (BIANCO, AFFUSO, PREITE 2021, pg. 135).

10. 4. Earrings
Bronze.
Intact.
Diam. 2.3 cm; bar: thick. 0.2 cm (inv. 324269); diam. 2.2 cm; bar: thick. 0.1 cm (inv. 324272).
Very thin bar earrings, with a rectangular section, single-coiled (inv. 324269) and double-coiled (inv. 324272).
Bernalda-Metaponto (prov. of Matera). National Archaeological Museum of Metaponto. Inv. 324269, 324272.

10. 5. Bracelet
Bronze.
Intact.

Length 3.3 cm; diam. 7.97 cm; wire: thick. 0.3 cm.
Bracelet made of wire, with an elliptical section, with ten coils. The ends, flattened, are folded into a curl. The bracelet was found, together with the piece with spiral-shaped tubes (inv. 324262, 324263), still on the right forearm.
Bernalda-Metaponto (prov. of Matera). National Archaeological Museum of Metaponto. Inv. 324265.
Bibliography: Cf. CHIARTANO 1994, pg. 106, T. 184, A (vol. I), pl. 14, T. 184, A (vol. II); pg. 195, T. 240, G (vol. I), plate 38, T. 240, G (vol. II); pg. 201, T. 258, A (vol. I), plate 44, T. 258, A (vol. II); pg. 115, T. 288, C, plate 57, T. 288, C (vol. II).

10. 6. Bracelet
Bronze.
Intact.
Length 19 cm, diam. 0.9 cm (inv. 324262, 324263); large ring: diam. 2.6 cm (inv. 324264).
Bracelet made up of two cylindrical segments of wire, with a circular section, wrapped in a spiral. The two elements are set into a large ring with an elliptical section, within which a small wire ring, featuring a circular section and coiled in a spiral, is inserted. The bracelet was found, together with the spiral-shaped piece (inv. 324265), still on the right forearm.
Bernalda-Metaponto (prov. of Matera). National Archaeological Museum of Metaponto. Inv. 324262 (spiral), inv. 324263 (spiral), inv. 324264 (large ring and small ring).
Bibliography: Cf. CHIARTANO 1994, pg. 201, T. 258, B (vol. I), pl. 44, T. 258, B (vol. II); BIANCO ET AL. 1996, pgs. 43, 52, 53, nr. 1.6.25-27; NAVA ET AL. 1998, pgs. 238, 239, plate 6, fig. 22.

10. 7. Finger rings
Bronze.
Intact. Minor parts missing.
Diam. 2.7 cm, length 2.9 cm (inv. 324258); diam. 2.1 cm, length 2.7 cm (inv. 324259); diam. 1.9 cm, length 1.6 cm (inv. 324260); diam. 2.5 cm, length 2.8 cm (inv. 324261).
Four cylindrical digital rings of wire, with a circular section, wound in a spiral (inv. 324260: eight spirals; inv. 324258: thirteen spirals; invv. 324259, 324261: fourteen spirals).
Bernalda-Metaponto (prov. of Matera). National Archaeological Museum of Metaponto. Inv. 324258, 324259, 324260, 324261.

10. 8. Fibula
Second half of the 9th - first half of the 8th century BC
Bronze, iron.
Intact. Reassembled pin.
Length 19.2 cm; spiral: diam. 9.5 cm; wire: thick. 0.4 cm.
Double spiral fibula with a figure-eight connection, originally crafted from a single piece; straight pin with a circular section; wire caychplate, also circular in section, bent into a C-shape. Due to the ancient breakage of the spring, which lacked coiling, a repair was made by flattening the broken end and securing it to the spiral with an iron nail.
Bernalda-Metaponto (prov. of Matera). National Archaeological Museum of Metaponto. Inv. 324266.
Bibliography: the fibula for comparison falls into Type 431: Spectacled fibulae with figure-eight connection, one piece: LO SCHIAVO 2010, pg. 841, nr. 7662 (vol. 2), plate 628, no. 7662 (vol. 3).

10. 9. Fibula
Second half of the 9th - first half of the 8th century BC
Bronze.
Not intact. Without spring; pin not reassembled.
Length 14.9 cm; width 13.8 cm; wire: thick. 0.4 cm.
Fibula made with two pairs of spirals, crossed and superimposed, nailed in the centre. Each pair consists of a single wire, with a circular section, wrapped in two spirals connected by an oblique connection. In one pair, the wire in the centre of a spiral forms the pin, in the other the catchplate. In the centre, on the visible side, there is a circular plaque, with a laminar section, decorated with embossed motifs: a perimeter row of dots that borders four tangent semicircles with a small cup in the centre.
Bernalda-Metaponto (prov. of Matera). National Archaeological Museum of Metaponto. Inv. 324250.
Bibliography: the fibula for comparison falls into Type 445: Large four-spiral fibulae, Incoronata Type: Lo Schiavo 2010, pg. 866, nr. 7926 (vol. 2), plate 661, no. 7926 (vol. 3).

10. 10. Chalcophone
Bronze.
Not intact. Fractures and parts missing on bars and rings.
Length 8 cm, width 8.5 cm (inv. 324251); length 5.6 cm, width 4.6 cm (inv. 324252); diam. max cm 5 (invv. 324253-324255).
Pendant consisting of two fringes and three series of concentric rings. A fringe is formed by two bars, the lower one being fractured and grooved, with thirteen holes. Corresponding to these holes are thirteen cylindrical wire spirals with a circular section. The other fringe, lacking the lower bar, consists of an incomplete upper bar that is grooved and has seven holes. Corresponding to these holes are seven cylindrical wire spirals with a circular section. Between the two fringes were three groups of concentric rings: two groups with seven rings each, and one with six rings, all gradually decreasing in size and arranged in a conical shape.
Bernalda-Metaponto (prov. of Matera). National Archaeological Museum of Metaponto. Inv. 324251, 324252 (bars with tubes), invv. 324253-324255 (three sets of concentric rings).
Bibliography: Cf. Lo Porto 1969, pg. 143, fig. 28, 4, 8; Frey 1991, pg. 21, T. 97, plate 6, 11; pg. 24, T. 111, plate 18, 13; pg. 26, T. 120, plate 28, 6; pg. 27, T. 124, plate 32, 11; Chiartano 1994, pgs. 75, 76, T. 209, B1-B2, C (vol. I), plate 21, T. 209, B1-B2, C (vol. II); pg. 202, T. 258, H, I, N (vol. I), plate 45, T. 258, H, I, N (vol. II); Bianco et al. 1996, pgs. 43, 52, 53, nr. 1.6.13; Nava et al. 1998, pgs. 238, 239, plate 6, fig. 22.

Chalcophones, likely bronze musical instruments, are found exclusively in high-status female burials dating back to the 8th century BC in the coastal Ionian regions of Basilicata and Calabria. Various types have been documented, but all are characterised by the presence of bars with through-holes and small spirals. The pieces from the Basilicata contexts consist of two fringes of cylindrical spirals attached to four bars with rounded ends (two per fringe); these two fringes are separated by a series of concentric rings. The pieces from the contexts of Calabria, simpler and smaller in size, consist of a single fringe of spirals attached to two bars with curled ends. The chalcophone was typically placed near or on the deceased's pelvis, hanging from a belt and sometimes accompanied by other ornaments of the funerary attire. In the Basilicata contexts, a darker soil was discovered near the chalcophone, possibly indicating the decomposition of organic materials such as wood, leather, or fabric. In the Calabria contexts, traces of wood have been found near some pieces, leading to the hypothesis that small rigid wooden bars were present inside the spirals. It is likely that this instrument, used in ritual ceremonies where music played a leading role, had to be played by percussion: holding it with one hand and hitting it with the fingers in order to make it resonate (COLELLI, FERA 2013, PGS. 823-832; SALTINI SEMERARI, 2019, pgs. 23-26, fig. 6; BIANCO, COLELLI, PREITE, *in print*).

10. 11. Composite pendant
Bronze.
Intact (double spiral pendant); some parts missing (cylindrical plate pendant).
Length 7.8 cm; width 9.5 cm; spiral: diam. 4.5 cm.
Pendant composed of four elements: a double spiral pendant made of wire with a circular section, featuring a connecting loop, and a lamina-wrapped pendant, flared at both ends. The two pendants are joined by a small ring made of spiral-wound wire, which is then inserted into a suspension ring with a rhomboidal section.
The composite pendant was located, together with the six studs (inv. 324256), above the chalice (invv. 324251-324255).
Bernalda-Metaponto (prov. of Matera). National Archaeological Museum of Metaponto. Inv. 324257.

10. 12. Spoke phaleras
Bronze.
Intact.
Diam. 9,8 cm (inv. 324247); diam. 9,5 cm (inv. 324248); diam. 8,7 cm (inv. 324249).
Three phalerae consisting of three concentric rings, with an elliptical section, joined at four points by eight small segments. Two pieces (inv. 324247, 324249) have a small wire hook inserted into the last ring. Also present is a double-wire element folded at both ends, probably a further hook between the phalerae.
The three phalerae and their hooks probably constituted the pendants of a belt or the belt itself.
Bernalda-Metaponto (prov. of Matera). National Archaeological Museum of Metaponto. Inv. 324247, 324248, 324249.
Bibliography: Cf. Chiartano 1994, pg. 107, T. 184, B1-B4 (vol. I), plate 14, T. 184, B1-B4 (vol. II).

10. 13. Studs
Bronze.
Intact.
Diam. 1 cm.
Six spherical cap studs with internal hook.
The studs were placed, together with the composite pendant (inv. 324257), above the chalice (invv. 324251-324255).
Bernalda-Metaponto (prov. of Matera). National Archaeological Museum of Metaponto. Inv. 324256.

11. Pisticci (prov. of Matera), Incoronata area. Tomb 258
8th century BC
Rectangular shaft tomb (length 2.15 m; width 0.85 m), oriented NW-SE. Structure made with pebbles and sandstone slabs.
Inhumation burial of adult female individual lying in a foetal position on her left side; skull facing NW. The skeleton was isolated from the overlying accumulation of stones by a thick layer (about 20 cm) of sandy soil, deposited at the time the body was laid.

Excavations: Archaeological Superintendency of Basilicata, year 1982.
Bibliography: Chiartano 1994, pgs. 200-203 (vol. I), pg. 28, plate XII, Volume 258, pgs. 88, 89, plates 44, 45 (vol. II).

Grave goods

11. 1. Jug
Achromatic pottery. Yellow-pink purified clay. Hand-shaped vase.
Reassembled and integrated. Some parts missing; eroded surfaces.
H 16 cm; body: diam. max 18.8 cm.
Expanded body tending towards biconical. Thin, rounded rim; very flared lip; swollen neck marked by a subtle recess; rounded shoulder; slightly concave, profiled base; vertical handle with a circular section, extending from the lip to the upper half of the shoulder.
Bernalda-Metaponto (prov. of Matera). National Archaeological Museum of Metaponto. Inv. 282053.
Bibliography: Chiartano 1994, pg. 203, S (vol. I), plate 44, S (vol. II).

11. 2. Bowl
Achromatic pottery. Yellow-pink purified clay. Hand-shaped vase.
Reassembled and integrated. Some parts missing; eroded surfaces.
H 6.2 cm; body: diam. max 17.2 cm.
Rounded rim; recessed lip; rim shoulder; low bowl with rounded profile; profiled concave base. There are two oblique vertical plastic tab handles inside, set and close to the shoulder.
Bernalda-Metaponto (prov. of Matera). National Archaeological Museum of Metaponto. Inv. 282054.
Bibliography: Chiartano 1994, pg. 203, R (vol. I), plate 44, R (vol. II).

11. 3. Loom weight
Fine dark brown ware. Hand-shaped weight.
Intact; surfaces eroded in places.
H 5.2 cm; lower base: 4 cm x 3.5 cm.
Truncated pyramid shape with a through suspension hole.
Bernalda-Metaponto (prov. of Matera). National Archaeological Museum of Metaponto. Inv. 147451.
Bibliography: Chiartano 1994, pg. 202, O1 (vol. I), plate 44, O1 (vol. II).

11. 4. Loom weight
Fine dark brown ware. Hand-shaped weight.
Not intact, missing upper base; surfaces eroded in places.
Residual height 2.8 cm; lower base: 2 cm x 1.6 cm.
Truncated pyramid shape with a through suspension hole, preserved in half, under the upper base.
Bernalda-Metaponto (prov. of Matera). National Archaeological Museum of Metaponto. Inv. 147453.
Bibliography: Chiartano 1994, pg. 202, O3 (vol. I), plate 44, O3 (vol. II).

11. 5. Bracelet
Bronze, iron.
Intact (bracelet); six fragments: recomposed, not intact and incomplete (chains).
Bracelet: length 6 cm; ends: max diam. 9.2 cm; central part: diam. 8.5 cm.
Chain links: length 17.3 cm; length 16.4 cm; length 11.8 cm; length 10.3 cm; length 9 cm; length 5.4 cm; length 4.6 cm; diam. from 0.8 cm to 0.6 cm.

Cylindrical bracelet made of wire, with sixteen coils, with the ends flattened and folded into a curl. From each end hang two chains, made of bronze wire rings, double-meshed, hanging from larger rings. One chain is attached to a curl via a spiral ring (1.1 cm in diameter). The other chain, not directly connected, was likely linked to the other curl through an iron ring (0.5 cm in diameter), a portion of which remains inserted in the curl. Four more fragments of iron bar are inserted into some links of the chain.
Decoration engraved on the wrapped wire of the bracelet. Motif with 5/6 thin horizontal lines, repeated at regular distances.
The bracelet (invv. 147424, 147426) was worn on the right arm, in association with the bracelet (inv. 147425), located between the arm and the forearm.
Bernalda-Metaponto (prov. of Matera). National Archaeological Museum of Metaponto. Inv. 147424 (bracelet), inv. 147426 (chains).
Bibliography: CHIARTANO 1994, pg. 201, A (vol. I), plate 44, A (vol. II). Cf. FREY 1991, pg. 21, T. 97, plate 6, 10; pg. 27, T. 124, plate 33, 21; BIANCO ET AL. 1996, pgs. 43, 53, nr. 1.6.27.

11. 6. Bracelet
Bronze.
Intact (two spiral elements); recomposed from two fragments (one spiral element).
Length 22 cm; diam. 7.5 cm; spiral: diam. 0.9 cm.
Bracelet made up of three spirally wound wire elements.
The bracelet (inv. 147425) was inserted between the right arm and forearm, together with the bracelet (inv. 147424, 147426).
Bernalda-Metaponto (prov. of Matera). National Archaeological Museum of Metaponto. Inv. 147425. Bibliography: CHIARTANO 1994, pg. 201, B (vol. I), plate 44, B (vol. II).

11. 7. Finger ring
Bronze.
Intact.
Length 3.1 cm; diam. 2.1 cm.
Finger ring of spirally wound wire (fourteen coils) with pointed ends.
Bernalda-Metaponto (prov. of Matera). National Archaeological Museum of Metaponto. Inv. 147434.
Bibliography: CHIARTANO 1994, pg. 202, M (vol. I), plate 44, M (vol. II).

11. 8. Hand ring
Bronze.
Intact.
Length 3.1 cm; diam. 2.1 cm.
Hand ring of spirally wound wire (fourteen coils) with pointed ends.
Bernalda-Metaponto (prov. of Matera). National Archaeological Museum of Metaponto. Inv. 147434.
Bibliography: CHIARTANO 1994, pg. 202, M (vol. I), plate 44, M (vol. II).

11. 9. Toe rings
Bronze.
Intact.

Length 2.7 cm, diam. 1.4 cm (inv. 147429); length 2.5 cm, diam. 1.7 cm (inv. 316004); length 2.6 cm, diam. 1.8 cm (inv. 316005); length 2.6 cm, diam. 1.7 cm (inv. 316006); length 2.6 cm, diam. 1.7 cm (inv. 316007).
Five toe rings with spirally wound wire.
Bernalda-Metaponto (prov. of Matera). National Archaeological Museum of Metaponto. Inv. 147429, 316004-316007.
Bibliography: Chiartano 1994, pg. 203, F1-5 (vol. I), plate 34, F1-5 (vol. II).

11. 10. Belt in bronze lamina
Bronze.
Reassembled. Parts missing on the edges.
Length 58 cm; width 1.9 cm.
Belt made of very thin bar, with a rectangular section, with both ends folded into a hook. Presence of a small hole (diam. 0.9 cm) near one of the two hooks.
Decoration made with embossed dots. Zigzag motif composed of double segments, alternating with two horizontal rows and occasionally interspersed with a circle motif featuring a cross inside. The edges of the bar are bordered by rows of dots.
Bernalda-Metaponto (prov. of Matera). National Archaeological Museum of Metaponto. Inv. 147428.
Bibliography: Chiartano 1994, pg. 202, E (vol. I), plate 45, E (vol. II).

11. 11. Phalera with pendants
Bronze.
Phalera: diam. 5.8 cm; pendant with multiple rings: max diam. 2.2 cm (large ring), max diam. 1.7 cm (small ring).
Phalera consisting of three concentric rings, with a trapezoidal section, joined at four points by eight small segments. From the phalera, via a small spiral ring inserted into the outermost ring, hangs a multi-ring element, consisting of a larger ring into which three smaller rings are inserted.
The set (phalera with multiple-ring pendant) includes two other similar pendants, not attached to the phalera.
The phalera with a pendant of multiple rings was tucked into the belt (inv. 147428).
Bernalda-Metaponto (prov. of Matera). National Archaeological Museum of Metaponto. Inv. 147430.
Bibliography: Chiartano 1994, pg. 202, G1-3 (vol. I), plate 45, G1-3 (vol. II).

11. 12. Chalcophone
Bronze.
Not intact. Reassembled. Minor parts missing.
Bars (n. 1): length 7.4 cm, width 0.7 cm; cylindrical spirals: length 7.2-6.9-6 cm, diam. 0.4 cm (inv. 147432).
Bars (n. 2): length 7.4 cm, width 0.5 cm; whole cylindrical spiral: length 6 cm, diam. 0.4 cm (inv. 147431).
Rings (n. 3): diam. 3.2 cm (three pieces); diam. 2.7-2.6 cm (three pieces); diam. 2.1 cm (three pieces); diam. 1.8 cm (three pieces); diam. 1.5 cm (two pieces); diam. 1.3 cm (one piece); diam. 1.2 cm (two pieces).
The pendant consists of three components: 1) two bars with a rectangular section and rounded ends, each grooved and pierced by thirteen holes, with each hole corresponding to a cylindrical spiral; 2) two bars, also with a rectangular section and rounded ends, grooved and pierced by eleven holes, each hole corresponding to a cylindrical spiral; and 3)

Catalogue of the exhibits on display

eighteen rings of bar with a rhomboid section, found scattered in the vicinity of components 1 and 2. Based on comparisons with complete chalcophones that have been found, the rings, which would have separated components 1 and 2, have been reassembled into three groups, each consisting of six rings arranged in decreasing size.
Bernalda-Metaponto (prov. of Matera). National Archaeological Museum of Metaponto. Inv. 147432 (cylindrical bars and spirals); inv. 147431 (cylindrical bars and spirals); inv. 147436 (rings).
Bibliography: CHIARTANO 1994, pg. 202, H, I, N (vol. I), plate 45, H, I, N (vol. II).

11. 13. Suspension ring
Bronze.
Intact.
Diam. 3.7 cm.
Ring in bar with triangular section.
Bernalda-Metaponto (prov. of Matera). National Archaeological Museum of Metaponto. Inv. 147427.
Bibliography: CHIARTANO 1994, pg. 202, D (vol. I), plate 45, D (vol. II).

12. Pisticci (prov. of Matera), San Teodoro area. Tomb 581
First half of the 8th century BC
Rectangular shaft tomb (2.10 m in length and 1 m in width), oriented NE-SW, bordered with stones and pebbles of varying sizes, with a particular concentration on the southern side.
Inhumation burial of adult female individual, laid in a foetal position on her left side.
Excavations: Archaeological Superintendency of Basilicata, year 1988.

Selected grave good
12. 1. Gold Bracteate disc (Fig. 7)
Gold sheet.
Intact.
Diam. 5,4 cm; thick. 0,1 cm.
Gold leaf disc with a smooth hemispherical central part and a straight perimeter part; near the edge, there are two small holes for fastening to a ceremonial/funerary garment.
Embossed decoration on the straight perimeter (rim) features a pattern of four small cups, each encircled by a continuous series of stitches, evenly spaced. Near the edge, two closely spaced concentric circles, also formed by a continuous series of stitches, complete the design.
Bernalda-Metaponto (prov. of Matera). National Archaeological Museum of Metaponto. Inv. 316013.
Bibliography: GUZZO 1994, pgs. 26, 27, fig. 1; DE SIENA, PREITE 2016, pgs. 218, 221, fig. 24. Cf. bronze pieces: FREY 1991, pg. 26, T. 118, plate 24, 9; pg. 27, T. 124, plate 31, 14; CHIARTANO 1994, pg. 104, T. 178, L6 (vol. I), plate 12, T. 178, L6 (vol. II); pg. 168, T. 186, L (vol. I), plate 16, T. 186, L (vol. II); gold pieces: BIANCO ET AL. 1996, pgs. 43, 52, 53, nr. 1.6.7 (Valle Sorigliano, tomb 28); BIANCO, PREITE (*in print*), Valle Sorigliano, tombs 28, 52 (Cf. ICCD records); tomb 71 (unpublished).
Tursi (MT), Valle Sorigliano, T. 28, cat. ICCD15967924: https://catalogo.beniculturali.it/detail/ArchaeologicalProperty/1700085631, consulted on 22.02.2024
Tursi (MT), Valle Sorigliano, T. 52, cat. ICCD15754872: https://catalogo.beniculturali.it/detail/ArchaeologicalProperty/1700212008, consulted on 22.02.2024

7.

Found in prestigious female burials and typically positioned on the ceremonial or funerary garment between the shoulder and chest, the rare gold bracteate discs—modelled after the more common bronze ones—are distinctive ornaments of the Oenotrian communities in the Ionian sub-coastal region.

The smooth spherical type from the 8th century BC, which is the most common in the sub-coastal Oenotrian area, features two holes for securing it. This design is likely a local adaptation or refinement of the older trans-Adriatic model with a pointed cap, which includes an internal loop. The latter model has been documented only in Anglona-Valle Sorigliano to date (BIANCO, PREITE, *in print*).

13. Pisticci (prov. of Matera), Incoronata area. Tomb 235

Second half of the 9th - first half of the 8th century BC
Rectangular shaft tomb (length 1.95 m; width 1.00 m), oriented NW-SE. Structure made with pebbles (walls and roofing) and sandstone slabs (roofing and large slab located vertically to the NW, behind the head of the individual buried). The deposition plane is made with sandstone slabs. Inhumation burial of adult female; skeleton, poorly preserved, perhaps placed in a foetal position on the left side; skull facing NW.
Excavations: Archaeological Superintendency of Basilicata, year 1982.
Bibliography: CHIARTANO 1994, pgs. 188-191 (vol. I), pg. 26, plate X, T. 235, pgs. 75-78, plates 31-34 (vol. II).

Grave goods

13. 1. Jug
Achromatic pottery. Yellow-pink purified clay. Hand-shaped vase.
Reassembled and integrated. Some parts missing; surfaces eroded in places.
H 21.5 cm; rim: diam. 10 cm; body: max diam. 19.7 cm; base: diam. 9 cm.
Expanded body tending towards biconical. Thin, rounded rim; very flared lip; swollen neck with a slight recess; rounded shoulder; slightly concave base; vertical bar-shaped handle with an elliptical section, positioned between the lip and the upper half of the shoulder.
Bernalda-Metaponto (prov. of Matera). National Archaeological Museum of Metaponto. Inv. 145895.
Bibliography: CHIARTANO 1994, pg. 188, A (vol. I), plate 34, A (vol. II).

13. 2. Filter vase with spout
Late 9th century BC
Matt-painted pottery. Purified pink clay. Hand-shaped vase.
Reassembled and integrated; eroded surfaces; decoration visible in places.
H 8.8 cm; rim: diam. 10 cm; body: max diam. 10.2 cm; base: diam. 6.9 cm.
Globular body. Thinned rim with a slight step on the inside; very short vertical lip; flat base; bridge handle made of a ribbon with an elliptical section, attached to the rim. Semi-circular profile spout. On the shoulder, in correspondence with the spout, there are six holes.
Monochrome painted decoration in black. On the shoulder, a repeated motif features three overlapping corners positioned closely together, framed by two parallel horizontal bands that are spaced apart. Marginal band, visible in places, on the edge of the spout. On the handle, a series of horizontal, parallel and spaced segments.
Bernalda-Metaponto (prov. of Matera). National Archaeological Museum of Metaponto. Inv. 145904.
Bibliography: CHIARTANO 1994, pg. 189, C (vol. I), plate 34, C (vol. II). Cf. YNTEMA 1990, pg. 33, fig. 17, 6.

Seven loom weights placed next to the spouted filter vase

13. 3. Loom weight
Fine brown-blackish ware. Hand-shaped weight.
Intact with slight chipping on the corners of the lower base; surfaces eroded in places. Areas blackened by exposure to fire.
H 6 cm; lower base: 3 cm x 2.1 cm.
Truncated pyramid shape with a through hole for suspension under the upper base.
Relief decoration in the form of a cup on the upper base.
Bernalda-Metaponto (prov. of Matera). National Archaeological Museum of Metaponto. Inv. 145899.
Bibliography: Chiartano 1994, pg. 188, B4 (vol. I), plate 31, B4 (vol. II).

13. 4. Loom weight
Fine brown-blackish ware. Hand-shaped weight.
Not intact, missing upper base; surfaces eroded in places.
Residual height 5.2 cm; lower base: 3.2 cm x 2.8 cm.
Truncated pyramid shape with a through hole for suspension, preserved in half, under the upper base.
Decoration impressed on the four faces with a pseudo-meander motif and double perimeter lines; on the lower base, a cross motif impressed with notches.
Bernalda-Metaponto (prov. of Matera). National Archaeological Museum of Metaponto. Inv. 145901.
Bibliography: Chiartano 1994, pg. 189, B6 (vol. I), plate 31, B6 (vol. II). Cf. Frey 1991, pg. 26, T. 120; plate 29, 19; Maaskant Kleibrink 2003, pg. 69, base right fig.; pg. 70, fig. 21, 1-3; Kleibrink 2016, pgs. 189-203.

13. 5. Loom weight
Fine brown-blackish ware. Hand-shaped weight.
Reassembled and incomplete; surfaces eroded in places.
H 4 cm; lower base: 1.7 cm x 1.7 cm.
Truncated pyramid shape with a through hole for suspension, preserved in half, under the upper base.
Bernalda-Metaponto (prov. of Matera). National Archaeological Museum of Metaponto. Inv. 145903.
Bibliography: Chiartano 1994, pg. 189, B8 (vol. I), plate 31, B8 (vol. II).

13. 6. Loom weight
Fine brown-blackish ware. Hand-shaped weight.
Reassembled and incomplete, edges chipped; surfaces eroded in places.
H 6.7 cm; lower base: 3.6 cm x 2.5 cm.
Truncated pyramid shape with a through hole for suspension under the upper base.
Decoration impressed on the four faces with a pseudo-meander motif and double perimeter lines; on the upper base, a cross motif impressed with notches.
Bernalda-Metaponto (prov. of Matera). National Archaeological Museum of Metaponto. Inv. 147281.
Bibliography: Chiartano 1994, pg. 189, B9 (vol. I), plate 31, B9 (vol. II). Cf. Frey 1991, pg. 26, T. 120; plate 29, 19; Maaskant Kleibrink 2003, pg. 69, base right fig.; pg. 70, fig. 21, 1-3; Kleibrink 2016, pgs. 189-203.

13. 7. Loom weight
Pink purified clay. Hand-shaped weight.
Intact; surfaces eroded in places.
H 6.2 cm; lower base: 3.6 cm x 3.3 cm.

Truncated pyramid shape with a through hole for suspension, under the upper base.
Decoration impressed with cross motif on the upper base.
Bernalda-Metaponto (prov. of Matera). National Archaeological Museum of Metaponto. Inv. 145896.
Bibliography: CHIARTANO 1994, pg. 188, B1 (vol. I), plate 31, B1 (vol. II). Cf. Frey 1991, pg. 26, T. 120; plate 29, 19; KLEIBRINK 2016, pgs. 189-203.

13. 8. Loom weight
Orange-pink purified clay. Hand-shaped weight.
Intact; surfaces eroded in places.
H 4.8 cm; lower base: 3 cm x 2.2 cm.
Truncated pyramid shape with a through hole for suspension under the upper base.
Bernalda-Metaponto (prov. of Matera). National Archaeological Museum of Metaponto. Inv. 145897.
Bibliography: CHIARTANO 1994, pg. 188, B2 (vol. I), plate 31, B2 (vol. II).

13. 9. Loom weight
Orange-pink purified clay. Hand-shaped weight.
Intact with slight chipping on the corners of the lower base; surfaces eroded in places.
H 3.8 cm; lower base: 2.4 cm x 1.8 cm.
Truncated pyramid shape with a through hole for suspension under the upper base.
Bernalda-Metaponto (prov. of Matera). National Archaeological Museum of Metaponto. Inv. 145898.
Bibliography: CHIARTANO 1994, pg. 188, B3 (vol. I), plate 31, B3 (vol. II).

13. 10. Bracelet
Late 9th - first half of the 8th century BC
Bronze.
Reassembled. Some parts missing on the tape.
Length 12.6 cm; diam. 8.7 cm; ribbon: width 1.5 cm.
Bracelet made of very thin bar, with a median rib, with seven coils. The ends, tapered, are folded into a curl.
Herringbone decoration engraved on the entire ribbon; along the edges the motif is framed by two lines.
The bracelet (inv. 145906), together with two others (invv. 145909, 145907), was worn on the right arm.
Bernalda-Metaponto (prov. of Matera). National Archaeological Museum of Metaponto. Inv. 145906.
Bibliography: CHIARTANO 1994, pg. 189, E (vol. I), plate 32, E (vol. II).

13. 11. Bracelet
Bronze.
Nine fragments that can only be partially reassembled.
Longer fragments: length 11 and 10.5 cm; diam. from 0.8 cm to 0.6 cm.
Bracelet consisting of two wire elements, with a circular section, wrapped in a spiral. The two longer fragments are held together by a wrapped bronze wire.
The bracelet (inv. 145909) was worn between the right arm and forearm, together with two other bracelets (inv. 145906, inv. 145907).
Bernalda-Metaponto (prov. of Matera). National Archaeological Museum of Metaponto. Inv. 145909. Bibliography: CHIARTANO 1994, pg. 189, H (vol. I), plate 32, H (vol. II).

13. 12. Bracelet
Bronze.
Intact.
Length 13 cm; spiral-shaped cones: max diam. 7.6 cm.
Bracelet made of wire, with a semi-circular section, with twenty-two coils. The flattened ends are made of wire wrapped in a spiral to form a cone.
The bracelet (inv. 145907) was worn on the right forearm, together with two other bracelets (inv. 145906, 145909).
Bernalda-Metaponto (prov. of Matera). National Archaeological Museum of Metaponto. Inv. 145907. Bibliography: CHIARTANO 1994, pg. 189, F1 (vol. I), plate 32, F1 (vol. II).

13. 13. Bracelet
Bronze.
Intact. Minor parts missing.
Length 11.5 cm; diam. 7 cm; spiral cones: diam. 7 and 6 cm.
Bracelet made of wire, with a semi-circular section, with twenty coils. The flattened ends are made of wire wrapped in a spiral to form a cone.
The bracelet (inv. 145908) was worn in the left forearm.
Bernalda-Metaponto (prov. of Matera). National Archaeological Museum of Metaponto. Inv. 145908. Bibliography: CHIARTANO 1994, pg. 189, F2 (vol. I), plate 32, F2 (vol. II).

13. 14. Finger rings
Bronze.
Intact; slight deformation (inv. 145912). Not intact and incomplete (inv. 145957).
Length 4.4 cm, diam. 2.5 cm (inv. 145912); length 3.9 cm, diam. 1.9 cm (145913); length 1.5 cm, diam. 2 cm (inv. 145957).
Three cylindrical finger rings of spirally wound wire with pointed ends (inv. 145912: twenty spirals; inv. 145913: fifteen spirals; inv. 145957: seven spirals).
The ring (inv. 145913) is inserted into the phalanx.
Bernalda-Metaponto (prov. of Matera). National Archaeological Museum of Metaponto. Inv. 145912, 145913, 145957.
Bibliography: CHIARTANO 1994, pg. 189, L1-3 (vol. I), plate 33, L1-3 (vol. II).

13. 15. Finger ring
Bronze.
Fragmentary and incomplete.
Length 1.5 cm; diam. 2 cm.
Cylindrical digital ring of spirally wound wire.
Bernalda-Metaponto (prov. of Matera). National Archaeological Museum of Metaponto. Inv. 145912, 145913, 145957.
Bibliography: CHIARTANO 1994, pg. 190, O1 (vol. I), plate 33, O1 (vol. II).

13. 16. Toe rings
Bronze.
Intact. Minor parts missing.
Length 2 cm, diam. 1.6 cm (inv. 145914); length 2.2 cm, diam. 1.7 cm (inv. 145915); length 1.7 cm, diam. 1.5 cm (inv. 145916); length 2.7 cm, diam. 1.5 cm (inv. 145919); length 2.6 cm, diam. 1.4 cm (inv. 145920).
Five cylindrical toe rings with spirally wound wire.
The rings (inv. 145919, 145920) are inserted into the phalanges.
Bernalda-Metaponto (prov. of Matera). National Archaeological Museum of Metaponto. Inv. 145914, 145915, 145916, 145919, 145920.
Bibliography: CHIARTANO 1994, pg. 190, Q (vol. I), plate 34, Q (vol. II).

13. 17. Fibula
Second half of the 9th - first half of the 8th century BC
Bronze.
Not intact. Some parts missing on the spirals and on the connection.
Length 19 cm; spiral: diam. 9.5 cm.
Double spiral fibula with figure-eight connection; spiral of wire, with circular section; bar connection with quadrangular section; straight pin, with circular section. The ancient breakage of the spring, without coiling, and the wire catchplate necessitated a two-part repair. This involved securing the flattened ends of the broken spring and wire to the two spirals using bronze nails.
Bernalda-Metaponto (prov. of Matera). National Archaeological Museum of Metaponto. Inv. 145937.
Bibliography: CHIARTANO 1994, pg. 190, T (vol. I), plate 33, T (vol. II). The fibula for comparison falls into Type 431: Spectacled fibulae with figure-eight connection, one piece: LO SCHIAVO 2010, pg. 842, nr. 766 (vol. 2), plate 628, no. 7666 (vol. 3).

13. 18. Fibula
Second half of the 9th - first half of the 8th century BC
Bronze.
Intact. Some parts missing on the edges.
Length 10 cm; spirals: diam. 5.4 cm; circular plaque: diam. 4.7 cm.
Fibula made with two pairs of crossing, superimposed spirals, nailed in the centre. Each pair consists of a single wire, with a circular section, wrapped in two spirals connected by an oblique connection. In one pair, the wire in the centre of the spiral forms the pin, in the other the catchplate. At the centre of the visible side is a circular plaque with a laminar section, featuring embossed decorations. These include a perimeter row of dots that encircles three tangent semicircles, with a small cup in the middle.
Bernalda-Metaponto (prov. of Matera). National Archaeological Museum of Metaponto. Inv. 145938.
Bibliography: CHIARTANO 1994, pg. 190, S (vol. I), plate 33, S (vol. II). The fibula for comparison falls into Type 445: Large four-spiral fibulae, Incoronata Type: LO SCHIAVO 2010, pg. 866, nr. 7926 (vol. 2), plate 661, no. 7926 (vol. 3).

13. 19. Belt in bronze lamina
Bronze.
Reassembled; parts missing on the ribbon and along the edges.
Length 68 cm; width 6.3 cm; ring: diam. 8.7 cm.
Belt made of very thin bar, with a rectangular section, with one end bent and the other equipped with a hook fixed to the bar with a bronze nail. A ring is inserted between the two hooks. Along the edges of the bar there are, at regular distances, small holes for fixing it to a support made of perishable material, which has not been preserved.
Decoration made in relief with a row of bullae and a series of semicircles defined with small dots along the two edges.
The belt was associated with the eight bronze phalerae (inv. 145939-145946), probably used as pendants.
Bernalda-Metaponto (prov. of Matera). National Archaeological Museum of Metaponto. Inv. 145959.
Bibliography: CHIARTANO 1994, pg. 189, G (vol. I), plate 32, G (vol. II). Cf. FREY 1991, pg. 21, T. 97, plate 5; pg. 26, T. 120, plate 29, 7; See for composition of belt with phalerae: BIANCO ET AL. 1996, pgs. 43, 53, nr. 1.6.28.

13. 20. Spoke phaleras
Bronze.
Intact.

Diam. 8,3 cm (inv.145939); diam. 8,5 cm (inv. 145940); diam. 8,7 cm (inv. 145941); diam. 8,6 cm (inv. 145942); diam. 8,9 cm (inv. 145943); diam. 8,6 cm (inv. 145944); diam. 8,5 cm (inv. 145945); diam. 8,6 cm (inv. 145946).
Eight phalerae consisting of three concentric rings, with a trapezoidal section, joined at four points by eight small segments.
The eight phalerae hung from the belt (inv. 145959).
Bernalda-Metaponto (prov. of Matera). National Archaeological Museum of Metaponto. Inv. 145939-145946.
Bibliography: CHIARTANO 1994, pg. 190, M1-8 (vol. I), plate 32, M1-8 (vol. II). See for composition of belt with phaleras: BIANCO *ET AL.* 1996, pgs. 43, 53, nr. 1.6.28.

13. 21. Multiple Ring Pendants
Bronze.
Intact. Part missing on a ring.
Pendants with four rings (invv. 145939-145958). Large rings: diam. from 4.1 cm to 4.6 cm; small rings: diam. from 3 cm to 3.7 cm.
Pendant with three rings (inv. 145956). Large ring: diam. 4.2 cm; small rings: diam. 3.5 cm.
Ten pendants: nine consisting of an elliptical section ring, in which three trapezoidal section rings are inserted. The tenth pendant consists of a trapezoidal section ring, in which only two rhomboidal section rings are inserted.
The ten pendants decorated the belt (inv. 145959).
Bernalda-Metaponto (prov. of Matera). National Archaeological Museum of Metaponto. Inv. 145939-145946.
Bibliography: CHIARTANO 1994, pg. 190, N1-10 (vol. I), plate 32, N1-10 (vol. II).

13. 22. Double spiral pendant
Bronze.
Not intact; fracture and part missing on the loop.
Width 4.2 cm; spirals: diam. 2 cm.
Double spiral pendant made of wire, with a circular section, with a connecting loop.
Bernalda-Metaponto (prov. of Matera). National Archaeological Museum of Metaponto. Inv. 145921.
Bibliography: CHIARTANO 1994, pg. 190, U (vol. I), plate 33, U (vol. II).

13. 23. Fringe pendant
Bronze.
Intact (rings); incomplete (cylindrical elements).
Large rings: diam. 4.5 cm; small rings: diam. 3 cm.
Cylindrical elements: max length 12 cm; max diam. 0.6 cm.
Fringe pendant consisting of twelve groups of three concentric rings arranged in decreasing order. The large rings have a trapezoidal section (inv. 145932), while the small ones are mostly elliptical in section (inv. 145933). Associated with the twelve groups of rings are twelve other elements of wire, wound in a spiral (inv. 145936).
The fringe pendant also includes twelve smaller rings (diam. 1.6 cm)[1].
This pendant is likely to be identified as a chalcophone.
Bernalda-Metaponto (prov. of Matera). National Archaeological Museum of Metaponto. Inv. 145932, 145933, 145936.
Bibliography: CHIARTANO 1994, pg. 191, Y (vol. I), plate 31, Y (vol. II).

---

[1] Not exposed.

13. 24. Ornament with two concentric fused rings
Bronze.
Intact.
Diam. max 2.8 cm.
Circular element, perhaps a pendant or suspension support, consisting of two concentric rings.
Also associated with the circular element are fifty-eight bronze rings with a trapezoidal or elliptical section (diameter from 2.1 cm to 1.7 cm)[2]. The set was positioned in contact with the femurs and likely formed a complex ornament attached to the funerary garment.
Bernalda-Metaponto (prov. of Matera). National Archaeological Museum of Metaponto. Inv. 145930.
Bibliography: CHIARTANO 1994, pg. 190, P (vol. I), plate 33, P (vol. II).

NATIONAL ARCHAEOLOGICAL MUSEUM OF SIRITIDE

14. Guardia Perticara (prov. of Potenza), San Vito area. Tomb 223
Mid-8th century BC
Rectangular shaft tomb (2.05 m in length, 0.70 m in width), oriented NE-SW, bordered with stone slabs and pebbles, with some pebbles sporadically present on the earth covering. The burial was disturbed in ancient times by the construction of tomb 224, which disrupted both the skeleton and the grave goods.
Inhumation burial of an adult female, placed in a supine position. Due to the disturbance, only the lower limbs remained in their original position.
Excavations: Superintendency for Archaeological Heritage of Basilicata, year 1997.
Bibliography: NAVA ET AL. 1998, pg. 241.

Selected grave good
14. 1. Ankle bracelets with spiral appendages (fig. 8)
Mid-8th century BC
Bronze.
Intact.
H 32 cm; diam. max 9 cm; diam. min. 4.5 cm; bar: thick. 0.2 cm; spiral: diam. 4.7 cm, wire: diam. 0.3 cm.
Two cylindrical bar anklets, rectangular in section, with seven coils. The ends, in very narrow bar, with a rectangular section, are wrapped in a spiral.
Decoration engraved on the wrapped ribbon: continuous perimeter line bordering a sequence of triangles on a background of slanting segments; continuous zigzag patterns along the central part.
Policoro (prov. of Matera). National Archaeological Museum of Siris. Inv. 214593.
Bibliography: NAVA ET AL. 1998, pg. 132, plate 11; BIANCO 2011, pg. 67.

15. Guardia Perticara (prov. of Potenza), San Vito area. Tomb 399 (Cf. *supra* pg. 36, fig. 7)
First half of the 8th century BC
Rectangular shaft tomb (length 2.40 m; width 0.80 m), oriented NS, covered and delimited with stones.

---

[2] Not exposed.

8.

Inhumation burial of an adult female individual, placed in a supine position, with the skull facing S.
Excavations: Superintendency for Archaeological Heritage of Basilicata, year 1999.
Bibliography: Nava 1999, pg. 696.

Policoro (prov. of Matera). National Archaeological Museum of Siritide
Section with skeleton (length 1.61 m; width of upper limbs: 0.47 m) together with personal ornaments and funerary garments.
Restored and reassembled.
Never exhibited before.

Visible grave goods in the section
15. 1. Bronze helmet-shaped headdress (fig. 10) made of six spiral tubes, hemispherical cap studs, three discs with holes and chains of circular-section rings (inv. 215239).
The headdress, given its size and the number of elements composing it, is comparable to pieces found in female burials within the same necropolis: tomb 30 (first half of the 8th century BC) and tomb 392 (8th century BC).
Bibliography: the headdress has never been exhibited before but already included in the chrono-typological sequence: Bianco, Affuso, Preite 2021, pgs. 139, 140 (volume I), pgs. 496, 498, figs. 8, 10 (volume II); Cf. Bianco 2011, pg. 66.

15. 2. A four-spiral fibula with a decorated rhomboid plaque featuring concave sides at the centre of the intersection, made of bronze. The fibula was placed in the centre of the chest (inv. 215240).
The fibula, of large dimensions (15 cm x 15 cm), for comparison belongs to Type 449: Large four-spiral iron arched fibulae, Francavilla type, can be dated between the second half of the 9th and the first half of the 8th century BC.
Bibliography: Cf. Lo Schiavo 2010, pgs. 877, 878 (vol. I), plates 691-693 (vol. II).

15. 3. A double-spiral fibula with a figure-eight connection, composed of two bronze pieces. It features a support band with a rectangular section, single-coiled spring with rectangular section, a straight pin, and a short symmetrical catchplate (inv. 215241). The two spirals are nailed to the support band with fixing nails covered by iron studs. A long bronze chain is attached to the fibula (inv. 215244). Positioned on the left side of the chest.

15. 4. A double-spiral fibula with a figure-eight connection, composed of two bronze pieces. It features a support band with a rectangular section, single-coiled spring with rectangular section, a straight pin, and a short symmetrical cathcplate (inv. 215242). The two spirals are nailed to the support strap with fixing nails. Positioned on the left side of the chest.

15. 5. A double-spiral fibula with a figure-eight connection, composed of two bronze pieces. It features a support band with a rectangular section, single-coiled spring with rectangular section, a straight pin, and a short symmetrical catchplate (inv. 215243). The two spirals are nailed to the support band with fixing nails, one covered by an iron stud. A bronze pendant with a quadrangular section is inserted into the pin (inv. 215245). Positioned on the centre-left side of the chest.
The three fibulae (inv. 215241-215243) for comparison fall into Type 434: Spectacled fibulae with figure-eight connection and spring-loaded band support, dating back to the 8th century BC.
Bibliography: Cf. Lo Schiavo 2010, pg. 844 (vol. I), plates 632-634.

9.

15. 6. Bronze leech fibula, with double-coiled spring and straight pin (inv. 23.S384-1.041). The fibula is placed on the left side of the chest, under the double spiral fibula (inv. 215245).

15. 7. A composite bronze pendant (fig. 11) featuring a zoomorphic pendant in the form of a ram's protome, connected to a spiral bronze tube with a glass paste bead, two biconical beads made of spirally wound wire, and a bronze chain (inv. 215248). The pendant is placed under the left hand. Bibliography. Ram protome: Cf. MAZZEI 2010, pg. 78, b, 1-2; double protome of rams: Cf. TABONE 1996, pg. 92, plate II, 11; NAVA ET AL. 1998, pg. 131, plate 10; BIANCO 2011, pg. 33; AFFUSO ET AL. 2012, pgs. 354, 256, fig. 2, nrs. 2, 3.

15. 8. Bronze disc with through hole (inv. 215246) placed on the pelvis as the central element of a belt made of perishable material.

15. 9. Bronze pin (inv. 23.S384-1.040) placed on the right side of the pelvis.

15. 10. Four spiral-shaped iron digital rings (inv. 215247) found on the fingers of the left hand.

15. 11. Two spiral-shaped iron digital rings (inv. 23.S384-1.042) found on the fingers of the right hand.

15. 12. Faceted biconical spindle whorl made of ware ceramic (inv. 215250) placed at the level of the left hand.

15. 13. Bronze pendant composed of two concentric circles with a circular section, containing five small rings inside: four linked together and one separate (inv. 215249). The pendant is placed on the outside of the left hand.

15. 14. Two biconical pendants made of spirally wound bronze wire (inv. 215251) located on the outside of the right tibia and left tibia.

15. 15. Two bronze rings with a thickened circular section (inv. 215252) located on the outer edge of the right tibia and left tibia.

15. 16. Three spiral-shaped bronze rings (inv. 215253) placed on the toes of the right foot.

15. 17. Three spiral-shaped bronze rings (inv. 215254) placed on the toes of the left foot.

The grave goods also include three matt-painted ceramic vases, recomposed and restored. The three vases, placed at the foot of the skeleton, are: a dipper juglet, an olla and a small olla. The first two have a brown painted decoration with a not very advanced curtain motif which, on the basis of comparisons (CERZOSO, VANZETTI 2014, pg. 258, cat. 979, pg. 347, plate 59, 979), allows a dating within the first half of the 8th century BC. This chronology is in substantial agreement with what is indicated by the bronze fibulae.

16. Chiaromonte (prov. of Potenza), Sotto la Croce area, property of De Marco. Tomb 110 (Cf. *supra* pg. 32-33, fig. 4-5)

Early 6th century BC
Shaft tomb (length 2.90 m; width 1.30 m), oriented EW.

10.

Inhumation burial of an adult male individual, placed in a supine position, with the skull facing west.
The area of the skeleton between the neck and the legs was covered by a thin layer of brown soil containing lumps of charcoal, likely resulting from the decomposition of perishable materials such as fabric or leather, possibly from a cloak. Traces of small perforated bone disks were also visible on this layer.
Excavations: Archaeological Superintendency of Basilicata, year 1986.
Bibliography: DE PALMA 1987, pgs. 690-694; BIANCO ET AL. 1996, pgs. 134-141.

Selected grave goods
16. 1. *Oinochoe*
Matt-painted pottery. Beige-pink purified clay. Wheel-thrown vase.
Reassembled and largely intact; painted decoration largely worn away.
H (with handle) 30.5 cm; rim: length 11 cm, width 10.5 cm, thick. 0.2 cm; neck: diam 6.6 cm; body: h 28 cm, max diam. 22 cm; foot: diam. 9.5 cm; handles: thick. 1.3 cm.
Pear-shaped body. Thinned rim; trilobate lip; concave neck with a plastic recess at the junction to the shoulder; rounded shoulder; truncated conical ring foot with a flat base; vertical double-bar handle extending from the rim/lip to the shoulder.
Two-tone painted decoration in black and reddish-brown, featuring horizontal bands of varying widths. Neck and handle filled with colour.
Policoro (prov. of Matera). National Archaeological Museum of Siritide. Inv. 210491.
Bibliography: BIANCO ET AL. 1996, pgs. 136, 137, nr. 2.9.17.

16. 2. *Thymatherion*
Matt-painted pottery. Beige-pink purified clay. Wheel-thrown vase.
Reassembled; painted decoration largely worn away.
H 28 cm; rim: diam. 8.6 cm, thick. 0.4 cm; body/trunk: max diam. 8.9 cm, min diam. 6.45 cm; foot: diam. 13.1 cm; handles: width 2.1 cm, thick. 0.7 cm.
Cylindrical body with swollen upper part. Rounded rim; flared lip; short concave neck; expanded foot; vertical ribbon-shaped handles, rectangular in section, set from the rim/lip to the shoulder.
Two-tone painted decoration in black and red-brown, poorly preserved and not definable in the decorative schemes. Flexible decoration: moulding placed on the joint between the trunk and the foot. Engraved decoration: on the trunk and foot, six thin horizontal and spaced lines, three above and three below the plastic moulding.
Policoro (prov. of Matera). National Archaeological Museum of Siritide. Inv. 210503.
Bibliography: BIANCO ET AL. 1996, pgs. 136, 137, nr. 2.9.29.

16. 3. Cup on high foot
Matt-painted pottery. Beige-pink purified clay. Wheel-thrown vase.
Reassembled; painted decoration largely worn away.
H 21.5 cm; rim: diam. 24 cm, thick. 0.55 cm; body: max diam. 26 cm; foot: diam. 14.2 cm; handles: thick. 1.5 x 1.35 cm.
Spherical body. The rim is slanted on the inside with a recessed, rounded lip. The vessel features a high, trumpet-shaped foot and oblique horizontal handles with a circular section, attached to the lip. Additionally, two flexible handles are positioned at the junction of the lip and bowl, alternating with the handles.
Two-tone painted decoration in black and red-brown.

External surface: traces of red-brown colour on the rim and lip; on the bowl, a series of semi-circular red bands outlined in black; on the foot, a pattern of three horizontal red bands outlined in black, spaced evenly.
Internal surface: on the base, a radial design featuring four tangent arches in red-brown, outlined by a series of black dots on the perimeter. At the centre of the motif is an unglazed circle decorated with a six-spoke radial pattern in black.
Handles: traces of black.
Policoro (prov. of Matera). National Archaeological Museum of Siritide. Inv. 210494.
Bibliography: BIANCO ET AL. 1996, pg. 136, nr. 2.9.16.

16. 4. Flask (Cf. *supra* pg. 34, fig. 6)
Third quarter of the 8th century BC
Cast and hammered bronze.
Reassembled and integrated.
H 32 cm; body: diam. 23.5 cm, width 8.5 cm, lamina: thick. 0.15 cm; spout: h 8.5 cm, diam. 2.9 x 2.4 cm, lamina: thick. 0.12 cm.
Bivalve lenticular body. Cylindrical spout with a tapered rim and short flared lip, made of wrapped lamina and nailed in the upper half with a bronze nail. Vertical handle in bar, with a quadrangular section, set on the upper part of the front plate; the flattened ends are fixed to the plate with bronze nails, of which only one remains.
Embossed decoration with concentric geometric motifs. On the body: double or single band motifs with dots alternating with single bands filled with vertical or oblique segments; in the centre, a large bulla.
Policoro (prov. of Matera). National Archaeological Museum of Siritide. Inv. 211161.
Bibliography: BIANCO ET AL. 1996, pgs. 88, 99, 138, nr. 2.9.41; BOTTINI 2007, pg. 141; BOTTINI 2020, pgs. 140, 141, figs. 1a-b.
Etruscan-Tarquinian production (Tarquinia). The flask, dated to the third quarter of the 8th century BC, but found among the grave goods of tomb 110, which dates to the early 6th century BC, illustrates the practice of hoarding particularly significant metal artefacts. It also highlights the longstanding connections between the inland Oenotrian region and the Tyrrhenian area (BOTTINI 2020, pg. 140).

16. 5. *Olpe*
Cast and hammered bronze.
Reassembled and incomplete.
H 21 cm; rim: diam. 6.5 cm, thick. 0.1 cm; body: diam. 8.86 cm; foot: diam. 6.3 cm.
Ovoid body made in lamina. Thinned rim; very flared lip; truncated conical neck; hollow truncated conical foot with flat support. Vertical ribbon-shaped handle with raised edges, featuring two longitudinal mouldings in the centre, extending from the lip to the widest part of the body. The upper attachment is cast, while the lower one is secured with nails.
The plastic decoration consists of two moulded cylinders: one positioned at the upper attachment of the handle and the other above the expansion of the ribbon near the lower attachment.
Policoro (prov. of Matera). National Archaeological Museum of Siritide. Inv. 210531.
Bibliography: BIANCO ET AL. 1996, pgs. 87, 99, 138, nr. 2.9.42.

16. 6. *Kotyle*
Cast and hammered bronze, lead.

Reassembled and incomplete.
H 11 cm; rim: width 12 x 10.5 cm, thick. 0.2 cm; foot: diam. 4.8 cm; handle: diam. 0.35 cm.
Cylindrical-ovoid body made of lamina. Flat rim, thickened on the inside; truncated conical foot filled with lead and featuring a flat base; horizontal wire handles with a circular section, attached to the body with bronze nails; the wire is flattened at the points of attachment.
Policoro (prov. of Matera). National Archaeological Museum of Siritide. Inv. 210478.
Bibliography: BIANCO ET AL. 1996, pgs. 87, 97, 138, 140, nr. 2.9.43; LOOTS 2020, pgs. 142, 150, plate 2, e; BOTTINI 2023, pg. 449, fig. 2.

16. 7. Basin on tripod
Cast and hammered bronze, forged iron.
Reassembled and incomplete.
H 27.5 cm; rim: diam. 22.5 cm, thick. 0.25 cm; omphalos: diam. 6 cm; supports: h 26.5 cm, thick. 0.85 cm.
Spherical body made of bronze lamina (thick. 0.1 cm). Flat rim, thickened on the inside; omphalos.
The basin was converted into a tripod by adding three wrought iron supports. These supports are made of bars with a quadrangular section, featuring expanded upper ends and outward-curving lower ends (feet). The three supports are each attached to the basin with two iron nails.
Policoro (prov. of Matera). National Archaeological Museum of Siritide. Inv. 210479.
Bibliography: BIANCO ET AL. 1996, pgs. 97, 138, 140, nr. 2.9.44; BOTTINI 2020, pg. 142.

16. 8. *Phiale*
Cast and hammered bronze.
Reassembled and very incomplete.
H 3.3 cm; rim: diam. 17.5 cm, thick. 0.3 cm; omphalos: diam. 3.9 cm; wall: thick. 0.15 cm.
Spherical body made of bronze lamina (thick. 0.1 cm). Flat rim, thickened on the inside; omphalos. Under the rim there are two small, close-together through holes.
Embossed decoration consisting of two bands, irregularly horizontal and spaced, filled with close vertical/oblique segments.
Policoro (prov. of Matera). National Archaeological Museum of Siritide. Inv. 210530.
Bibliography: this piece has never been exhibited before. The decoration with engraved strokes, similar to that reproduced on the flask (cat. 16. 4, below), finds a possible comparison with that present on another *phiale* from Chiaromonte, Sotto la Croce area, Tomb 68: TAGLIENTE 1985, pg. 178, plate 3, 7; BOTTINI 2023, pgs. 449, 450, fig. 5.

16. 9. "Corinthian" helmet
Cast and hammered bronze, forged iron.
Reassembled and incomplete.
H 21.1 cm; cap: length 23 cm, width 18.5 cm; base: length 27.5 cm, width 19.5 cm; lamina: thick. 0.1 cm; nose guard: thick. 0.4 cm.
Helmet, with a slightly pronounced top, an ellipsoidal profile, and slightly inward-curving walls at the nape; narrow neck guard; slightly pronounced cheekpieces; thick nasal guard; eye openings with a triangular outline.
On the top of the cap, the iron fixing points of the *lophos* are preserved. The edges of the helmet are lined with a series of small holes for the leather padding.

Policoro (prov. of Matera). National Archaeological Museum of Siritide. Inv. 210479.
Bibliography: BIANCO ET AL. 1996, pgs. 119, 121, 138, 139, nr. 2.9.49.

16. 10. Right arm and forearm protection elements
Cast and hammered bronze.
Armguard: length 31 cm; width 16 cm; diam. 15 cm; thick. 0.18 cm; forearm guard: length 30 cm; width 12 cm; diam. 12 cm; thick. 0.18 cm.
Reassembled (armguard); recomposed and incomplete (missing forearm).
Anatomically modelled tubular sheet elements. The armguard features a broad expansion and upper curvature of the plate, distinctly defined in the lower section by two oblique grooves meeting at an angle. This design allowed for adequate mobility of the humerus and shoulder. The lower end of the armguard is shaped with a deep curve at the elbow. The upper edge of the armguard features two mouldings, one along the perimeter and a second more internally, with single or paired series of through holes in the intermediate space for padding attachment. The remaining edge is smooth, with a series of small, evenly spaced through holes, also intended for securing the leather padding. The forearm, less anatomically characterised, does not have any through holes along the edge.
Policoro (prov. of Matera). National Archaeological Museum of Siritide. Inv. 211165 (armguard), inv. 211164 (forearm).
Bibliography: BIANCO ET AL. 1996, pgs. 120, fig. on the left, 121, 139, nr. 2.9.51; BOTTINI 2020, pg. 146, fig. 6.

16. 11. Right shin guard
Cast and hammered bronze.
Right shin guard: h 41 cm; calf: max. width 16 cm, min. width 10.5 cm; thick. 0.2.
Anatomically shaped tubular lamina element.
The edges of the shin guard are outlined by a series of small holes for the leather padding.
Policoro (prov. of Matera). National Archaeological Museum of Siritide. Inv. 211163.
Bibliography: BIANCO ET AL. 1996, pgs. 120, fig. on the right, 121, 139, nr. 2.9.50.

16. 12. Left shin guard
Cast and hammered bronze.
Left shin guard: h 40 cm; calf: max. width 16 cm, min. width 13; thick. 0.2 cm.
Anatomically shaped tubular lamina element.
The edges of the shin guard are marked by a series of small holes for the leather padding.
Policoro (prov. of Matera). National Archaeological Museum of Siritide. Inv. 211163.
Bibliography: BIANCO ET AL. 1996, pgs. 120, fig. on the right, 121, 139, nr. 2.9.50.

16. 13. *Machaira* with scabbard
Wrought iron, bone/ivory, wood.
Reassembled and incomplete (*machaira*); some parts missing (knife).
Machaira: length 54 cm; blade: max. width 5.25 cm, min. width 3.9 cm, max. thick. 1.15 cm, min. thick. 0.75 cm; hilt: width 6.8 x 6.65 cm, thick. 0.4.
Knife: length 63.5 cm; width 3.5 cm.
A weapon with an iron blade featuring an elongated triangular section; the back is slightly curved with a flat upper profile; sinuous cut; the blade broad-

ens at mid-length and tapers near the tip. Grip-tongue sword-style hilt, wider and curved at the end, with ivory heel and handguards. The blade is inserted in a wooden scabbard. Some remains of the wooden scabbard.
On the *machaira* is an iron knife with bone/ivory heels fixed with iron nails, oxidated. Some remains of wood on the blade of the knife.
Policoro (prov. of Matera). National Archaeological Museum of Siritide. Inv. 11168, 211167 (*machaira*), 211168 (knife).
Bibliography: BIANCO ET AL. 1996, pgs. 139, 140, nr. 2.9.52.

16. 14. Spearhead
Forged iron.
Reassembled and incomplete.
Length 51.7 cm; blade: length 40.4 cm, max. width 4.4 cm, thick. 0.4 cm; handle: length 11.3 cm, base: width 1.15 x 1.2 cm; diam. 2.5 cm, thick. 0.35 cm.
A very long spearhead in foliated lamina, featuring three longitudinal central ribs bordered by deep lateral grooves; the handle is hollow and cylindrical, with a rhomboid section at the base, transitioning to a circular section towards the end.
Residues of the wooden shaft inside the handle. On the spearhead there is a residue of perishable material, perhaps fabric.
The spearhead is associated with the butt spike (inv. 211169).
Policoro (prov. of Matera). National Archaeological Museum of Siritide. Inv. 211160.
Bibliography: BIANCO ET AL. 1996, pgs. 139, 140, nr. 2.9.54.

16. 15. Spear Butt Spike
Forged iron.
Reassembled and incomplete.
Length 27.5 cm; thick. 0.5 x 0.5 cm; handle: diam. 1.9 cm.
Bar butt spike, with a quadrangular section, with a hollow cylindrical handle, with a circular section.
The butt spike is associated with the spearhead (inv. 211160).
Policoro (prov. of Matera). National Archaeological Museum of Siritide. Inv. 211169.
Bibliography: BIANCO ET AL. 1996, pgs. 139, 140, nr. 2.9.56.

16. 16. Javelin tip
Forged iron.
Reassembled.
Length 39.8 cm; blade: length 14.5 cm, max. width 3.5 cm, thick. 0.4 cm; handle: length 25.3 cm, width 1.05 x 1.1 cm; base: diam. 2.6 cm, thick. 0.35 cm.
A tip in foliated lamina featuring a triple longitudinal central rib and a long hollow cylindrical handle with a circular section.
Policoro (prov. of Matera). National Archaeological Museum of Siritide. Inv. 211159.
Bibliography: BIANCO ET AL. 1996, pgs. 139, 140, nr. 2.9.55.

16. 17. Horse bit
Forged iron.
Reassembled.
Length 22 cm; width 16.5; bar: diam. 1 cm; tie shafts: bar length 11.5-12 cm, thick. 0.65 x 0.65 cm, ring diam. 2.8.
Jointed fillet made up of two twisted bars with lateral eyelet terminations. The two bars are connected at the central eyelets (joint) and are attached via the lateral eyelets to two additional bars with C-shaped ends (bridles). These bridles feature three eyelets on the back: one central (hook) and two lateral ones, evenly spaced.

There are two straight bar elements with a quadrangular section, featuring an eyelet at one end and a slightly curved tip at the other (tie shafts).
Policoro (prov. of Matera). National Archaeological Museum of Siritide. Inv. 210483.
Bibliography: Bianco et al. 1996, pgs. 139, 141, nr. 2.9.58.

16. 18. Andirons
Forged iron.
Reassembled and incomplete.
Andiron 1: length 23 cm; width 1 cm; thick. 0.35 cm. Andiron 2: length 24.4 cm; width 1 cm; thick. 0.35 cm.
Two andirons made of bar with a quadrangular section, featuring ends that widen into an elliptical shape; the opposite ends, which are significantly narrowed, are made of rectangular-section bars bent upwards. Residues of the attachments of the U-shaped supports are preserved.
Policoro (prov. of Matera). National Archaeological Museum of Siritide. Inv. 210480.
Bibliography: Bianco et al. 1996, pgs. 139, 141, nr. 2.9.60.

16. 19. Spit
Forged iron.
Reassembled and incomplete.
Length 38 cm; bar: width 0.65 x 0.55 cm; head: h 3 cm, width 2 cm; thick. 0.2
Spit made in bar, with an irregular quadrangular section, with a diamond-shaped head, with a rectangular section.
Policoro (prov. of Matera). National Archaeological Museum of Siritide. Inv. 210481.
Bibliography: Bianco et al. 1996, pgs. 139, 141, nr. 2.9.61.

17. Guardia Perticara (prov. of Potenza), San Vito area. Tomb 380
Mid-8th century BC
Rectangular shaft tomb (length 1.45 m; width 0.80 m), oriented NS. The burial was disturbed in ancient times.
Inhumation burial of an individual, adult female, placed in a supine position. Poorly preserved skeleton
Excavations: Superintendency for Archaeological Heritage of Basilicata, year 1999.
Never exhibited before

Selected grave good
17. 1. Helmet-shaped headdress
Mid-8th century BC
Bronze.
Not intact. Reassembled.
H 18.5 cm; length 25 cm; width 18.5 cm.
Helmet-shaped headdress made up of thirteen spiral tubes, hemispherical cap studs, four discs with holes and a pendant with circular section rings.
Policoro (prov. of Matera). National Archaeological Museum of Siritide. Inv. 212255.
Bibliography: the headdress has never been exhibited before but already included in the chrono-typological sequence: Bianco, Affuso, Preite 2021, pgs. 139, 140 (volume I), pgs. 496, 498, figs. 8, 10 (volume II).

The helmet-shaped headdresses with discs and chains, whose typology could derive from Balkan prototypes (Bianco 2011, pg. 65), documented only in the Oenotrian necropoleis of San Vito (Guardia Perticara, prov. of Potenza) and

Spirito Santo area (Chiaromonte, prov. Potenza), are composed of "*a series of overlapping spiral-shaped tubes wrapped around the head, with the upper cap decorated with large bronze studs. The set of overlapping tubes and studs had to be applied to a single fabric or leather support. In this type as well, the tubes are connected at the back by prominent elements in the form of bronze discs made of lamina with small holes, while another disc is positioned at the top of the cap.*" (BIANCO, AFFUSO, PREITE 2021, pg. 136).

18. Chiaromonte (prov. of Potenza), Spirito Santo area. Tomb 349
Mid-8th century BC
Rectangular shaft tomb (length 2.90 m; width 0.90 m), oriented NS, bordered with stone slabs and pebbles, sporadically also present on the earth covering.
Inhumation burial of an adult female, placed in a supine position, with the skull facing north.
Excavations: Archaeological Superintendency of Basilicata, year 1995.
Bibliography: BOTTINI 1995, pg. 629.

Selected grave good
18. 1. Helmet-shaped headdress (Cf. *supra* pg. 37, Chiaromonte)
8th century BC
Bronze.
Not intact. Reassembled.
H 18 cm; length 25 cm; width 18 cm.
Helmet-shaped headdress made up of ten spiral tubes, hemispherical cap studs, four discs with holes and a pendant with rings, with a circular section.
Policoro (prov. of Matera). National Archaeological Museum of Siritide. Inv. 23.S384-1.043.
Bibliography: the headdress has never been exhibited before but already included in the chrono-typological sequence: BIANCO, AFFUSO, PREITE 2021, pgs. 139, 140 (volume I), pgs. 496, 498, figs. 8, 10 (volume II).

19. Aliano-Alianello (prov. of Matera), Cazzaiola area. Tomb 316
Second half of the 8th century BC
Rectangular shaft tomb (length 2.55 m; width 1.30 m), oriented EW.
Inhumation burial of an adult female individual, placed in a supine position, with the skull facing west.
Excavations: Archaeological Superintendency of Basilicata, year 1984.
Bibliography: BOTTINI 1984, pg. 499, plate XXVIII, 1; BIANCO *ET AL.* 1996, pgs. 152-154; NAVA *ET AL.* 1998, pg. 245.

Selected grave good
19. 1. Semi-circular tube headdress (fig. 11)
Second half of the 8th century BC
Bronze.
Not intact. Reassembled.
Length 52 cm.
Semi-circular headdress made of sixteen spiral-shaped tubes of wire with a circular section. Inside the tubes, some fragments of willow twigs were found.
"*The headdress is constructed at the base with horizontal spiral tubes that are overlapping and continuous, some of which form a front-to-back connection on the head through folds. The horizontal basal tubes curve upwards at the ends at an acute angle, forming a sharply arched*

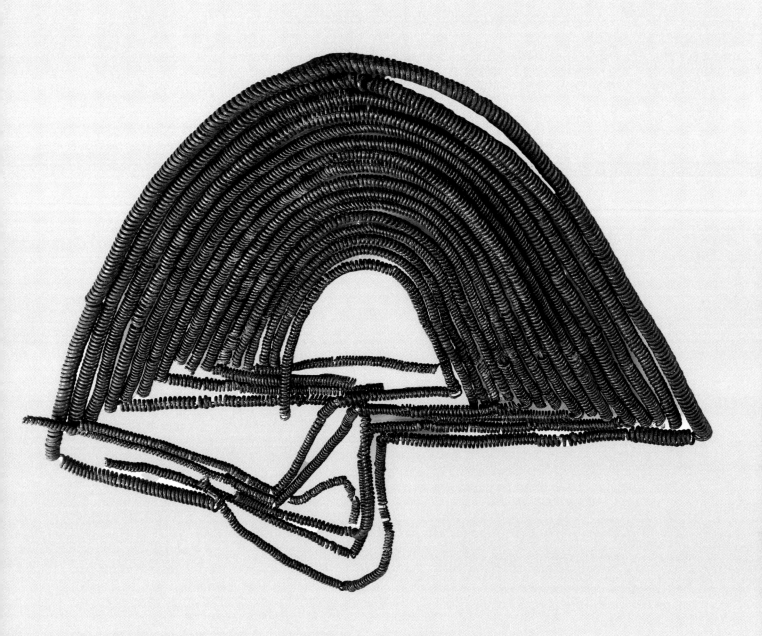

semicircle that is positioned vertically on the head. The basic structure was likely inserted into a fabric support that served as a base, while the tubes arranged in a vertical semicircle, typically numbering 16-18, were kept in shape by thin, flexible willow branches inserted inside them, fragments of which have been found." (BIANCO, AFFUSO, PREITE 2021, pg. 136).
Policoro (prov. of Matera). National Archaeological Museum of Siritide. Inv. 205366.
Bibliography: NAVA ET AL. 1998, pg. 148, plate 27; BIANCO, AFFUSO, PREITE 2021, pg. 140 (volume I), pg. 495, figs. 7, 8, 10 (volume II).

20. Guardia Perticara (prov. of Potenza), San Vito area. Tomb 514 (fig. 12)
First half of the 7th century BC
Rectangular shaft tomb, destroyed on the E side (length 0.80 m; width 0.70 m), oriented EW.
Inhumation burial of an adult female individual, lying in a supine position.
Excavations: Superintendency for Archaeological Heritage of Basilicata, year 1999.
Bibliography: BIANCO 2000, pgs. 24, 25, fig. 12.

Selected grave goods
20. 1. Large ceremonial fibula
Bronze.
Intact.
Length 35 cm; catchplate: length 7 cm, width 2 cm, thick. 0.2 cm.
Large simple skene arch fibula in bar, rectangular in section; single-coiled spring, rectangular in section; slightly curved pin, circular in section; asymmetrically expanded cathcplate, embossed with a series of dots arranged in a triple perimeter row and a large zigzag pattern, created with a double row of dots extending across the plate.
Four bronze rings of different sizes are inserted into the pin, with a circular, rhomboidal and elliptical section.
Policoro (prov. of Matera). National Archaeological Museum of Siritide. Inv. 215829.
Bibliography: BIANCO 2000, pg. 49, cat. 28; BIANCO 2011, pg. 51.

20. 2. Large ceremonial fibula
First half of the 7th century BC
Bronze, bone.
Intact.
Length 29 cm.
Large simple skene arch fibula in bar, rectangular in section, covered with two large quadrangular bone beads; double-coiled spring with a circular section; slightly curved pin with a circular section; long, asymmetrical catchplate with a serrated edge.
Policoro (prov. of Matera). National Archaeological Museum of Siritide. Inv. 215828.
Bibliography: BIANCO 2000, pg. 49, cat. 27; BIANCO 2011, pg. 51. The fibula for comparison falls into Type 171: Large covered arch fibulae and long catchplate: LO SCHIAVO 2010, pg. 388, nr. 2833 (vol. I), plate 204, nr. 2833 (vol. II).

20. 3. Composite belt in bronze, amber, ivory (fig. 13)
Bronze, amber, ivory.
Intact.
Length 100 cm; bronze disc: diam. 8.5 cm, thick. 0.2 cm.

12.

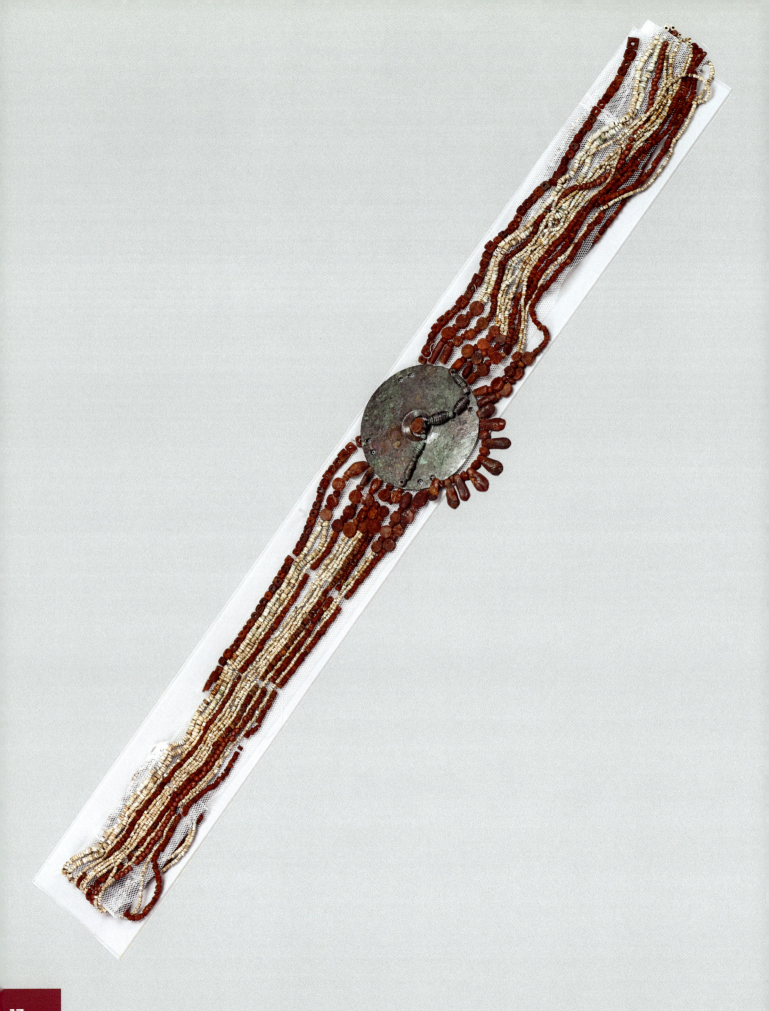

Belt made of alternating rows of ivory and amber beads; the upper and lower rows (edges) are made with only quadrangular amber beads. At the centre, there is a bronze disc with a shaped central hole, with an amber bead inside, from which hang cylindrical spirals of bronze wire and amber pendants. The disc also features four pairs of small through holes, placed along the edge, perhaps for attachment to the perishable material support of the belt.
Policoro (prov. of Matera). National Archaeological Museum of Siritide. Inv. 215837.
Bibliography: BIANCO 2000, pg. 49, cat. 36; BIANCO 2011, pg. 51.

20. 4. Pendant in the shape of a bird (fig. 14)
Bronze.
Intact (plaque); incomplete (chain links).
Plaque: h 7.4 cm; length 15 cm; width 7 cm; thick. 1.5 cm.
Pendant consisting of a rectangular plaque in the shape of a stylised ornithomimus. There are a series of holes on the lower edge of the upper limbs and the plate for inserting chain links.
Decoration engraved with small lines and thin zigzag motifs and small squares.
It has a metal bar with bent end, perhaps without pendant, soldered through oxidation on the bronze mesh.
Policoro (prov. of Matera). National Archaeological Museum of Siritide. Inv. 215838.
Bibliography: BIANCO 2000, pg. 49, cat. 37; BIANCO 2011, pg. 51.

20. 5. Studs
Bronze.
Intact.
Diam. 0.6 cm.
Nine triangular sets consisting of hemispherical cap studs with internal loop. The sets constituted decorative elements of the funerary dress.
Policoro (prov. of Matera). National Archaeological Museum of Siritide. Inv. 215840.
Bibliography: BIANCO 2000, pg. 49, cat. 38; BIANCO 2011, pg. 51.

20. 6. Composite necklace in amber and *faïence* (fig. 15)
Amber, *faïence*.
Length 14 cm; length 20 cm; length 28 cm.
Composite necklace consisting of three necklaces of varying and graduated sizes, featuring bulla and trapezoidal pendants made of amber, with flattened spherical amber beads spaced along the two smaller necklaces. The largest necklace, in addition to the bulla and trapezoid pendants in amber, features five Egyptian figures, one of which depicts the god Bes (length 3.5 cm) in *faïence*.
Policoro (prov. of Matera). National Archaeological Museum of Siritide. Inv. 215809.
Bibliography: BIANCO 2011, pg. 51.

21. Chiaromonte (prov. of Potenza), Sotto la Croce area. Tomb 96
Early 6th century BC
Shaft tomb (length 2.59 m; width 0.90 m), oriented EW.
Inhumation burial of an adult female individual, placed in a supine position, with the skull facing west.
Excavations: Archaeological Superintendency of Basilicata, year 1985.

Selected grave good
21. 1. Amber necklace with pendant in the shape of a female head (fig. 16; Cf. *supra* pg. 38, fig. 9)

15.

Early 6th century BC
Amber.
Intact.
Length 25.8 cm; pendant with female head: length 4 cm; pendant with scaraboid: length 15.5 cm; scaraboid: length 4.8 cm.
Composite necklace made up of four wires, of different and scalar sizes, with bulla pendants and spherical beads. Connected to the necklace, perhaps with a wire of amber beads, is a pendant in the form of a female protome in the Daedalian style, with large eyes and a nose covering the mouth, hair with wavy edges and a truncated cone-shaped headdress. The composite necklace also includes a pendant made up of eight beads, one oblong and seven lenticular ones, and a pendant shaped like a scarab (scaraboid).
Policoro (prov. of Matera). National Archaeological Museum of Siritide. Inv. 211770 (necklace), inv. 210442 (female protome), inv. 211769 (elongated pendant).
Bibliography: BIANCO 2005A, pg. 45, fig. left (female protome), pg. 100 (composite necklace); BIANCO 2020, pgs. 122, 123, fig. 22.

22. Chiaromonte (prov. of Potenza), Sotto la Croce area. Tomb 154 (figs. 17-18)
Early 6th century BC
Rectangular shaft tomb (length 2.60 m; width 0.85 m), oriented EW.
Inhumation burial of an adult female, placed in a supine position, with the skull facing west.
Excavations: Superintendency for Archaeological Heritage of Basilicata, year 1988.
Bibliography: NAVA ET AL. 1998, pg. 243, plates 21-23.

Selected grave goods
22. 1. *Aryballos*
Pottery. Beige-pink purified clay. Wheel-thrown vase.
Reassembled. Part missing on the rim and lip.
H 6.3 cm; rim: diam. 0.9 cm; lip: width 1.1 cm; body: max diam. 6.9 cm.
Globular body. Rounded rim; wide rim lip; short cylindrical neck; flat base. Vertical ribbon-shaped handle set from lip to top of shoulder.
Policoro (prov. of Matera). National Archaeological Museum of Siritide. Inv. 213143.
Never exhibited before.

22. 2. Ointment jar
Achromatic pottery. Purified beige-pink clay. Wheel-thrown vase.
Reassembled.
H 17 cm; rim: diam. 1.5 cm; body: max diam. 14 cm.
Globular body. Thinned rim; flared lip; sub-cylindrical neck (h 4.5 cm); foot profiled in the shape of a pomegranate.
Policoro (prov. of Matera). National Archaeological Museum of Siritide. Inv. 213137.
Never before exhibited.

22. 3. Bowl
Achromatic pottery. Beige-pink purified clay. Wheel-thrown vase.
Reassembled. Some parts missing on the rim and lip.
H 7 cm; width 19 cm.
Single-handled bowl. Slanted rim on the inside; recessed lip; truncated cone-shaped bowl; flat base. Oblique horizontal handle, with a circular section, set on the lip.

17.

Policoro (prov. of Matera). National Archaeological Museum of Siritide. Inv. 213104.
Never exhibited before.

22. 4. Cup on foot
Achromatic pottery. Beige-pink purified clay. Wheel-thrown vase.
Reassembled. Some parts missing on the rim and lip.
H 5 cm; rim: diam. 9 cm; body: max diam. 11 cm.
Cup on foot.
Policoro (prov. of Matera). National Archaeological Museum of Siritide. Inv. 213120.
Never exhibited before.

22. 5. Cup on foot
Achromatic pottery. Purified beige-pink clay. Wheel-thrown vase.
Reassembled. Some parts missing on the rim and lip.
H 3.5 cm; rim: diam. 5.5 cm; body: max diam. 6.5 cm; foot: diam. 4 cm.
Cup on foot.
Policoro (prov. of Matera). National Archaeological Museum of Siritide. Inv. 213121.
Never exhibited before.

22. 6. Bracelet
Bronze.
Not intact. Parts missing and widened at one end.
Length 14.5 cm; diam. 10 cm.
Bracelet made of wire, with an elliptical section, with multiple coils. The ends are folded into a curl.
Policoro (prov. of Matera). National Archaeological Museum of Siritide. Inv. 213166.
Bibliography: NAVA ET AL. 1998, pg. 143, plate 21.

22. 7. Silver and amber earrings
Silver, amber.
Intact.
Diam. 5 cm.
Pair of small earrings made of silver wire wrapped in a spiral with overlapping and decorated ends. Both pieces feature a flattened spherical amber bead.
Policoro (prov. of Matera). National Archaeological Museum of Siritide. Inv. 213147.
Bibliography: NAVA ET AL. 1998, pgs. 142, 143, plate 21, 22; BIANCO 2020, pg. 124, fig. 23.

22. 8. Silver and amber ornaments
Silver, amber.
Intact.
Diam. 10.8 cm; diam. 9 cm.
Pair of large ornamental elements made of spirally wrapped silver ribbon with overlapping ends. The ribbon is decorated with pointed triangles (a sawtooth pattern). One piece contains three amber beads, while the other contains only two. Found in succession, after the earrings (inv. 213147), could be interpreted as pendant earrings, originally attached to a ribbon made of perishable material or as a braid holder.
Policoro (prov. of Matera). National Archaeological Museum of Siritide. Inv. 213146.

Bibliography: Nava *et al.* 1998, pgs. 142, 143, plate 21, 22; Bianco 2020, pg. 124, fig. 23.

22. 9. Gold necklace
Gold.
Minor parts missing.
Length 25.5 cm.
Necklace consisting of spherical beads. The central part is designed with eleven series of five spherical beads alternating with a flask-shaped bead.
Policoro (prov. of Matera). National Archaeological Museum of Siritide. Inv. 213148.
Bibliography: Nava *et al.* 1998, pg. 143, plate 21.

22. 10. Necklace of silver, amber, and glass paste
Silver, amber, glass paste.
Intact.
Length 18.5 cm.
Necklace composed of amber beads in various shapes: circular, bulla-shaped with an upper appendage, and flask-shaped in both amber and silver; as well as circular blue glass paste beads adorned with white eyes and yellow dots.
Policoro (prov. of Matera). National Archaeological Museum of Siritide. Inv. 213160.
Never exhibited before.

22. 11. Composite Amber Necklace
Amber.
Intact.
Outer necklace: length 122 cm; inner necklace: length 105 cm; largest central bead: 2.5 cm; smallest bead: 0,5 cm.
Composite necklace made up of four necklaces, of different sizes and scalar, with pendants of various shapes and sizes: spherical-flattened; acorn-shaped; heart-shaped; bulla-shaped; ovoid. The beads are distinguished by an upper appendage featuring a cleft with a passing hole.
Policoro (prov. of Matera). National Archaeological Museum of Siritide. Inv. 213161.
Bibliography: Nava *et al.* 1998, pg. 143, plate 21.

22. 12. Silver fibula with pendant
Silver. Minor parts missing.
Max length 12 cm; arch: width 2.5 cm.
Fibula with a thickened, slightly depressed arch of circular section, featuring three cylindrical nodules bordered by two ribs; single-coiled spring with circular section; straight pin, also of circular section; and a short, symmetrical catchplate. A double-wired silver pendant with two spherical beads with a small cone at the base end is inserted onto the pin.
Policoro (prov. of Matera). National Archaeological Museum of Siritide. Inv. 213149.
Bibliography: Nava *et al.* 1998, pgs. 143, 144, plates 21, 23. Cf. with bronze pieces: Lafli, Buora 2006, pgs. 38, 43, nr. 15, plate XIV, e) (first half of the 7th century BC); Lo Schiavo 2010, pgs. 232, 234 (vol. I), plate 101, 1340 B-1340 G (vol. II), the fibula for comparison falls into the Class of Greek and Greek-Oriental arched fibulae, in types 87-88; Verger 2014, pgs. 15-21 (with previous bibliography), in particular, pg. 20, for the fibula from Tomb 154: Phrygian-inspired fibulae of northern Greek or southern Balkan production (second half of the 7th century BC). Cf. with gold pieces: Ignatiadou 2012, pg. 394, fig. 8, pg. 404, cat. 13 (end of VI century BC / 525-500 BC).

22. 13. Amber pendant
Amber.
Intact.
H 6.5 cm; width 4.5 cm.
Pendant composed of a trapezoidal bead topped by a circular bead with a lenticular section; at the base of the trapezoidal bead, four pendants are attached, each consisting of spherical beads with a trapezoidal bead at the end.
Policoro (prov. of Matera). National Archaeological Museum of Siritide. Inv. 213170.
Bibliography: NAVA ET AL. 1998, pg. 143, plate 21.

22. 14. Ceremonial apron with amber ornaments
Amber.
Intact.
Length 67 cm; width 45 cm.
Decorative element composed of two strands of spherical beads with a lenticular section, varying in size, and ovoid beads with a lower apex.
The two amber strands formed the border of a ceremonial apron, originally made of organic material, of which no trace remains.
Policoro (prov. of Matera). National Archaeological Museum of Siritide. Inv. 213162.
Bibliography: NAVA ET AL. 1998, pg. 143, plate 21.

23. Policoro (prov. of Matera), Madonnelle area, Colombo property. Tomb 11
(Cf. *supra*, pg. 37)
Early 7th century BC
Burial at *enchytrismos* consisting of an amphora[3], cut in half by the plough. Inside the amphora (urn) there is a small skull in fragments, some teeth and small rib fragments. The grave goods, found outside, consist of a miniature *kalathos*, two small Phrygian fibulae near the skull and three astragals.
Excavations: Archaeological Superintendency of Basilicata, year 1977.
Bibliography: BERLINGÒ 2017, pg. 111, fig. 3, nr. 11.

Grave goods
23. 1. Miniature *Kalathos*
7th century BC
Pottery. Beige purified clay, wheel-thrown.
Intact; colour peeling in places.
H 1.7 cm; rim: diam. 5.5 cm; lip: thick. 0.4 cm; base: diam. 3.05 cm.
Truncated conical bowl. Slightly oblique rim on the outside; pseudo-rim lip; flat base.
Decoration painted in dark brown with reddish streaks on both surfaces.
Policoro (prov. of Matera). National Archaeological Museum of Siritide. Inv. 49652.
Bibliography: BERLINGÒ 2017, pg. 111, nr. 13, fig. 3, nr. 11.
Probable Chiota production.

23. 2. Fibulae
Bronze.

---

[3] Amphora of Corinthian production, Type A: Berlingò 2017, pg. 111.

Intact; some parts missing on the catchplates.
1) h 2 cm; width 2.5 cm; arch: diam. 0.25 cm, decorative knot diam. 0.45 cm; pin: diam. 0.1 cm.
2) h 1.7 cm; width 2.45 cm; arch: diam. 0.2 cm, decorative knot diam. 0.4 cm; pin: diam. 0.1 cm.
Fibulae featuring a thickened arch of circular section, adorned with three cylindrical nodules and covered by seven or eight thin ribs; triple-coiled spring with a circular section; straight pin, also of circular section; symmetrical catchplate with a rectangular plate, slightly tapered at the base, with a high back. The catchplate features two expanded tongues at the junction with the anterior arch and a very short lower fold.
Policoro (prov. of Matera). National Archaeological Museum of Siritide. Inv. 49654.
Bibliography: Berlingò 2017, pg. 111, nr. 14, fig. 3, nr. 11. The fibulae fall into Type 88: Fibulae with a thickened arch and decorated with three narrow cylindrical ribbed nodules, Siris type: Lo Schiavo 2010, pgs. 232, 234 (vol. I), plate 101, 1340 E, 1340 F (vol. II). Cf. Malnati 1985, pg. 76, 3, plate XX, B, 3; Verger 2014, pgs. 15-21 (with previous bibliography), in particular, pg. 20, for the two fibulae from Tomb 11: Phrygian-type fibulae, made in Ionia or at *Polieion*, dating back to the second half of the 8th and the first half of the 7th century BC.
The type was produced in pairs (Lo Schiavo 2010, pg. 233) and the two pieces were probably placed, as clasps, on the funerary garment, at shoulder height (Berlingò 2017, pg. 111). The morphological analysis of the two fibulae, considering the lateral arrangement of the triple coils of the springs and the side of the very short lower fold of the catchplates (Preite, description *infra*), suggests that they must have been positioned in a symmetrical and specular manner, according to the Greek model (Verger 2014, pg. 20).

23. 3. Three astragals
Bone.
Intact; surfaces slightly eroded.
1) length 3 cm; width 1.5 cm;
2) length 2.8 cm; width 1.5;
3) length 1.5 cm; width 0.7 cm.
Policoro (prov. of Matera). National Archaeological Museum of Siritide. Inv. 49653.
Bibliography: Berlingò 2017, pg. 111, nr. 15, fig. 3, nr. 11.

24. Policoro (prov. of Matera), Madonnelle locality, Colombo property. Tomb 48 (Cf. *supra*, pg. 24, fig. 7)
Mid-7th century BC
Burial at *enchytrismos* consisting of an amphora[4], placed in a horizontal position, with a pebble fixed near the base, perhaps as a support, found at a depth of 1.86 m from ground level. Within the amphora lie the remains of an individual, possibly an infant, with a preserved rib fragment and a tooth, accompanied by grave goods consisting of a Rhodian cup and two iron fibulae.
Excavations: Archaeological Superintendency of Basilicata, year 1980.

---

[4] Amphora of Chalcidian production, Type SOS: Berlingò 2017, pg. 127.

Catalogue of the exhibits on display

Bibliography: Berlingò 1986, pg. 123, plate 18; Berlingò 2017, pg. 127, fig. 11, nr. 48.

24. 1. Amphora
Pottery. Pink purified clay. Wheel-thrown vase.
Reassembled and incomplete; colour partially faded.
H 70 cm; rim: diam. 18.8 cm, thick. 2 cm; body: diam. 42 cm, thick. 0.4 cm; foot: diam. 10.6 cm; handle: 3.1 x 2.8 cm.
Ovoid body tapering downwards. Thickened banded rim; cylindrical neck; low, hollow, truncated cone-shaped foot; vertical handles with an elliptical section, extending from the neck to the shoulder. At the junction between the rim and the neck, extending over the handles, there is a thin, smooth tongue cord.
Decoration painted in black and reddish spots with geometric motifs. Rim, thin smooth cord, body, foot and handles filled with colour. On the neck, unglazed: a motif composed of two pairs of horizontal parallel lines, spaced apart, with the intervening space filled by a metope frame featuring three concentric circles with a central dot, flanked by a double vertical *a tremolo* line on each side.
Policoro (prov. of Matera). National Archaeological Museum of Siritide. Inv. 47067.
Bibliography: Berlingò 2017, pg. 127, nr. 56, fig. 11, nr. 48.
Chalcidian production. The piece is the only example of an amphora, Type SOS, of Chalcidian production currently documented in the western necropolis of the Madonnelle area (Berlingò 2017, pg. 127).

Selected grave goods
24. 2. Cup
Pottery. Beige-pink purified clay. Wheel-thrown vase.
Reassembled and fragmentary, missing a handle; partially flaking paint.
H 6.35 cm; rim: diam. 12.5 cm; body: max diam. 12.5 cm, thick. 0.35 cm; foot: diam. 4.1 cm; handle: diam. 0.7 cm.
Thinned rim; slightly flared lip; rounded shoulder; hemispherical-flattened bowl; hollow, truncated conical foot; horizontal, slightly oblique handles with a circular section, attached at the shoulder.
Reddish-brown painted decoration covering both surfaces of the cup, with the exception of an unglazed band between the handles.
Policoro (prov. of Matera). National Archaeological Museum of Siritide. Inv. 47068.
Bibliography: Berlingò 2017, pg. 127, nr. 57, fig. 11, nr. 48.
Probable Aegean production.

25. Policoro (MT), Madonnelle area, Colombo property. Tomb 92
Second half of the 7th century BC
Burial by *"incineration in a pit"* (Berlingò 1993, pg. 15).
Excavations: Archaeological Superintendency of Basilicata, year 1981.
Bibliography: Lattanzi 1981, pg. 274; Berlingò 1993, pg. 15.

Accessory
25. 1. Small jug
Fine grey ware pottery. Wheel-thrown vase.
Intact. Parts missing on the rim/lip; eroded surfaces.
H (with handle) 5.7 cm; h (without handle) 5.1 cm; rim: diam. 4.75 cm; body: max diam. 5.2 cm, wall thick. 0.35 cm; foot: diam. 3.4 cm; handle: diam. 1 cm.
Ovoid body. Slanted rim on the inside; flared lip; concave neck; flat base; vertical handle, with a circular section, set from the rim/lip to the middle of the body.

Policoro (prov. of Matera). National Archaeological Museum of Siritide. Inv. 200538.
Bibliography: Berlingò 1993, pgs. 15, 19, fig. 33.

25. 2. Small jug
Dark beige fine ware pottery. Wheel-thrown vase.
Reassembled and integrated. Parts missing on the rim/lip; eroded surfaces.
H (with handle) 8 cm; h (without handle) 6 cm; rim: diam. 4.1 cm; body: max diam. 5.25 cm, wall thick. 0.4 cm; handle: width 1.6 cm, thick. 0.7 cm.
Globular body. Slanted rim on the inside; slightly flared lip; cylindrical neck; rounded base; vertical ribbon-shaped handle with slight longitudinal saddle, rectangular section, set by the rim/lip at the maximum expansion of the body.
Policoro (prov. of Matera). National Archaeological Museum of Siritide. Inv. 200539.
Bibliography: Berlingò 1993, pgs. 15, 19, fig. 33.

25. 3. Protocorinthian *oinochoe*
Pottery. Beige purified clay. Wheel-thrown vase.
Reassembled and integrated; colour at times faded and chipped.
H (with handle) 9.4 cm; h (without handle) 8 cm; opening; length 5.6 cm, width 5.6 cm; body: max diam. 8.85 cm, wall thick. 0.3 cm; foot: diam. 8.8 cm; handle: handle: width 1.7 cm, thick. 0.6 cm.
Truncate cone-shaped body. Thinned rim; trilobate lip; cylindrical neck; very short distinct ring-shaped foot with flat support base; vertical ribbon-shaped handle, with rectangular section, set from the rim/lip to the shoulder.
Decoration painted in brown and engraved with geometric motifs. On the rim, lip, neck and handle: traces of colour. On the shoulder: two large, spaced, horizontal and parallel bands of colour with the intermediate space decorated with a repeating petal motif, made with an engraved perimeter line. On the body: a series of colour-filled bands/background; along the lower edge of the body: an unglazed band decorated with a horizontal pattern of evenly spaced brown dots.
Policoro (prov. of Matera). National Archaeological Museum of Siritide. Inv. 200536.
Bibliography: Berlingò 1993, pgs. 15, 19, fig. 33.

25. 4. Proto-Corinthian pyx with lid
Pottery. Beige purified clay. Wheel-thrown vase.
Reassembled and integrated. Some parts missing on the edge; colour flaking in places.
H (with lid) 12.8 cm; pyx: h 7 cm, rim diam. 10.65 cm, wall thick. 0.35 cm; base: diam. 11.25 cm; lid: diam. 11 cm; knob: h 4.5 cm, max diam. 3.25 cm, min diam. 1.6 cm.
Cylindrical body with a slightly concave profile. Thinned and rounded rim; flat base; horizontal handles, with a circular section, set under the rim. Disc-shaped lid, with a truncated conical handle knob, connected via a small cylinder, with a circular interlocking strip inside for closing.
Two-tone painted decoration in brown and red with geometric motifs.
Pyx, external surface: a pattern consisting of three horizontal sets of three thin, parallel lines in brown, alternating with three horizontal parallel bands in brown. On the body, there are three sets of four horizontal, parallel plastic mouldings, each outlined by thin brown lines. On the handles: traces of brown colour. Inner surface: dark red background.
Lid: two concentric circular bands, spaced apart, in red and reddish-brown, with brown edges. Knob: motif of horizontal, parallel bands in red-

dish-brown, edged in brown. The top of the knob is unfinished and features a circular recess with a small cylinder in the centre, possibly intended to hold a decorative element that is no longer present.
Policoro (prov. of Matera). National Archaeological Museum of Siritide. Inv. 200535.
Bibliography: Berlingò 1993, pgs. 15, 19, fig. 33.

25. 5. Miniature cup
Pottery. Beige purified clay. Wheel-thrown vase.
Reassembled. Some parts missing; eroded colour.
H 3 cm; rim: diam. 6.3 cm; wall: thick. 0.25 cm; foot: diam. 2.5 cm; handles: diam. 0.5 cm.
Thin, rounded rim; slightly flared lip; dome-shaped bowl; cylindrical foot; horizontal handles with a circular section positioned at the junction between the shoulder and the bowl.
Decoration painted in brown; traces of colour are visible on the internal surface.
Policoro (prov. of Matera). National Archaeological Museum of Siritide. Inv. 200540.
Bibliography: Berlingò 1993, pgs. 15, 19, fig. 33.

25. 6. Miniature bowl
Pottery. Orange purified clay. Wheel-thrown vase.
Reassembled. Parts missing on the rim; colour eroded in places.
H 3 cm; rim: diam. 5.5 cm; wall: thick. 0.25 cm; foot: diam. 2.5 cm; handle: width 0.55 cm, thick. 0.4 cm.
Thinned and rounded rim; slightly flared lip; dome-shaped bowl; ring foot; vertical strap handle with a rectangular section, extending from the rim/lip to the shoulder/bowl junction point.
Decoration painted in brownish colour. Traces of colour are visible on both surfaces.
Policoro (prov. of Matera). National Archaeological Museum of Siritide. Inv. 200537.
Bibliography: Berlingò 1993, pgs. 15, 19, fig. 33.

26. Policoro (MT), Madonnelle area, Colombo property. Tomb 115 (Cf. *supra*, pg. 22, fig. 6)
Mid-7th century BC
Burial at *enchytrismos* consisting of an amphora[5], placed in a horizontal position, oriented SW-NE. The amphora, not isolated, was placed near two other amphorae (nos. 114, 116).
Excavations: Archaeological Superintendency of Basilicata, year 1981.
Bibliography: Berlingò 1993, pg. 13, figs. 23, 25.

26. 1. Amphora
Pottery. Dark pink purified clay. Wheel-thrown vase.
Reassembled and incomplete; fragmentary foot; colour at times faded and chipped.
H (residual) 60 cm; rim: diam. 19 cm; neck: diam. 12.5 cm; body: max diam. 50, wall thick. 0.7 cm; handle: diam. 3 cm.
Ovoid body tapering downwards. Thickened banded rim; cylindrical neck; likely low, hollow, truncated cone-shaped foot; vertical handles

---

[5] Amphora of Attic production, Type SOS: Berlingò 1993, pg. 13.

with a circular section, extending from the neck to the shoulder. At the junction between the rim and the neck, extending over the handles, there is a thin, smooth tongue cord.
Decoration painted in red-brown with geometric motifs. Rim, thin smooth cord, shoulder, lower body, foot fragments and handles: filled with colour. On the neck, unglazed: a metope square featuring two concentric circles with a central dot, and on either side, a double, possibly triple, vertical *a tremolo* line in reddish-brown. On the body, under the lower attachment of the handles: motif of four thin, horizontal and parallel lines.
Policoro (prov. of Matera). National Archaeological Museum of Siritide. Inv. 205606.
Bibliography: BERLINGÒ 1993, pgs. 13, 19, figs. 23, 25.
Attic production.

27. Policoro (MT), Madonnelle area, Colombo property. Tomb 224 (Cf. *supra*, pg. 27, fig. 8)

Mid-7th century BC
Cremation burial consisting of a *hydria*[6], located in a horizontal position and oriented NW-SE.
Excavations: Archaeological Superintendency of Basilicata, year 1981.
Bibliography: BERLINGÒ 2000, pgs. 71, 74, nr. 2.

27. 1. *Hydria*

Pottery. Reddish purified clay. Wheel-thrown vase.
Reassembled and integrated; missing half of the neck. Colour faded or crusted in part.
H 42 cm; rim: diam. 19.2 cm, thick. 1.3 cm; neck: diam. 13 cm, thick. 0.65 cm; foot: diam. 11.5 cm; vertical handle: width 3.3 cm, thick. 1.55 cm; horizontal handles: diam. 1.7 cm.
Ovoid body tapering downwards. Thickened and rounded rim; flared lip; concave neck; hollow, truncated cone-shaped foot; vertical ribbon-shaped handle with an elliptical section, extending from the middle of the neck to the shoulder; oblique horizontal handles with a circular section, positioned at the widest part of the body.
Decoration painted in red-brown, with orange shades due to firing defects, with geometric motifs.
External surface. Rim, lip, upper part of the neck, lower end of the body, foot, and horizontal handles are filled with colour. On the neck: metopes featuring vertical *a tremolo* motifs, spaced apart and bordered below by three horizontal, parallel bands. On the shoulder: four motifs of six concentric semicircles with a small central dot, arranged at regular intervals, and bordered below by a wide horizontal band, followed by another band with a small unglazed space. On the body, at the level of the horizontal handles: two spaced series of four thin, horizontal, parallel lines, with the space between them filled by a serpentine horizontal band that ends near the handle attachments. On the lower body: four broad horizontal and parallel bands, separated by a small unglazed space. Vertical handle: two vertical bands and one horizontal band bordering the edges and lower attachment; two bands in the centre, joined in the middle, with ends that diverge and curve irregularly, forming a loop motif.

---

[6] *Hydria* of Cycladic production: Berlingò 2000, pg. 71.

Internal surface. On the rim and upper edge of the lip: background the same colour as the external surface.
Policoro (prov. of Matera). National Archaeological Museum of Siritide. Inv. 205635.
Bibliography: Berlingò 2000, pgs. 71, 74, nr. 2.
Cycladic production.

28. Guardia Perticara (prov. of Potenza), San Vito area. Tomb 502 (Cf. *supra*, pg. 39, fig. 11)

Early 6th century B.C
Shaft tomb (length 2.30 m; width 1.20 m), oriented EW, covered with earth mixed with pebbles and sandstone fragments. The burial was located under tomb 497. Context partly disturbed.
Inhumation burial of an adult female individual, placed in a position, presumably supine, with the skull, given the turmoil of the burial, located on the W side.
Excavations of the Superintendency for Archaeological Heritage of Basilicata 1999.
Bibliography: Nava 2000, pg. 957, plate XXXVI, 1; Bianco 2012, pgs. 239-247.

Selected grave goods
28. 1. Olla
Matt-painted pottery. Beige-pink purified clay. Wheel-thrown vase.
Reassembled with some parts missing; painted decoration mostly worn away.
H 26 cm; rim: diam. 16.8 cm; base: diam. 12 cm.
Globular body vase. Flat rim; everted lip; short neck with a raised cord at the base decorated with oblique notches; profiled base. Three symmetrical vertical triple-stick handles set from the cord to the shoulder.
Two-tone painted decoration in black and reddish-brown, featuring bands on the rim and shoulder, from which contrasting semi-circular motifs descend onto the body. Handles painted in red-brown.
Policoro (prov. of Matera). National Archaeological Museum of Siritide. Inv. 215907.
Bibliography: Bianco 2012, pg. 244.

28. 2. Olla
Matt-painted pottery. Beige-pink purified clay. Wheel-thrown vase.
Reassembled with some parts missing; painted decoration largely worn away.
H 25.4 cm; rim: diam. 23.7 cm; base: diam. 10.2 cm.
Globular body. Thinned and rounded rim; flared lip; truncated conical neck; profiled base. Four vertical handles, two of which are zoomorphic, and two with triangular tops and rectangular panels applied at mid-height, extending from the lip to the widest point of the body; two additional horizontal oblique handles with a circular section are set on the lower part of the body, below and aligned with the handles featuring rectangular panels.
Two-tone painted decoration in black and reddish-brown with geometric, phytomorphic and zoomorphic motifs. On the rim, there are radial motifs; on the neck, square motifs filled with a fine meander pattern; on the body, zoomorphic motifs flanked by phytomorphic motifs with rosettes. Handles decorated with red-brown fields accompanied by black bands and/or geometric motifs.
Policoro (prov. of Matera). National Archaeological Museum of Siritide. Inv. 215893.
Bibliography: Bianco 2012, pgs. 242, 243.

28. 3. *Stamnos* with lid
Matt-painted pottery. Beige-pink purified clay. Wheel-thrown vase. Reassembled; painted decoration largely worn away.
H 20.5 cm; internal rim: diam. 20.5 cm; lid: diam. 24 cm.
Large *stamnos* with an expanded, shaped body, distinguished by careens at the junction of the rounded shoulder and the deeply recessed base. Raised rim featuring a perimeter recess to accommodate the insertion of the lid; profiled base.
Hemispherical dome lid with flared and hollow handle knob.
Stamnos: two-tone painted decoration in black and reddish-brown, featuring horizontal bands and a large meander pattern on the body.
Lid: two-tone painted decoration in black and red-brown with horizontal bands.
Policoro (prov. of Matera). National Archaeological Museum of Siritide. Inv. 215911.
Bibliography: BIANCO 2012, pg. 244.

28. 4. Dipper Juglet
Matt-painted pottery. Beige-pink purified clay. Wheel-thrown vase. Reassembled with some parts missing.
H 5.9 cm; rim: diam. 6 cm; base: diam. 3.1 cm.
Ovoid body. Rounded rim; flared lip; profiled base. Vertical ribbon-shaped handle, overlapping, with upper eyelet, set from the lip to the point of maximum expansion of the body.
Monochrome painted decoration in brown. On the rim are radial motifs; on the neck a wide filled band; on the body a series of narrow bands with vertical lines.
Policoro (prov. of Matera). National Archaeological Museum of Siritide. Inv. 215894.
Bibliography: BIANCO 2012, pg. 243.

28. 5. *Kantharos*
Matt-painted pottery. Beige-pink purified clay. Wheel-thrown vase. Reassembled with parts missing; decoration partly worn away.
H 8.8 cm; rim: length 7.3 cm, width 6.8 cm; base: diam. 5 cm.
Flattened ovoid body. Rounded rim; straight lip; flattened mouth at the handles; truncated conical neck; flat base. Vertical ribbon-shaped handles, overlapping, set from the lip to the point of maximum expansion of the body.
Two-tone painted decoration in black and red-brown. On the rim, there are black transverse lines; on the neck, a series of alternating wide and narrow bands in reddish-brown and black; on the body, a motif of opposing semicircles with two small V-shaped lines inside, at the top, in black.
Policoro (prov. of Matera). National Archaeological Museum of Siritide. Inv. 215919.
Bibliography: BIANCO 2012B, pg. 245.

28. 6. *Kantharos*
Matt-painted pottery. Beige-pink purified clay. Wheel-thrown vase. Reassembled; decoration partly worn away.
H 18.6 cm; rim: length 14.5 cm, width 12.5 cm; base: diam. 7.5 cm.
Ovoid body. Rounded rim; flared lip; flattened mouth at the handles; truncated conical neck; profiled base. Vertical ribbon-shaped handles, overlapping, set from the lip to the point of maximum expansion of the body.
Two-tone painted decoration in black and reddish-brown featuring geometric, phytomorphic, and anthropomorphic motifs. On the rim, there

are radial motifs; on the neck, there are squares filled with a checkerboard pattern, rosette-shaped phytomorphic motifs in the achromatic squares, and meander-shaped motifs; on the body, there are stylized pseudo-hourglass-shaped anthropomorphic motifs, filled with thin bands and two-coloured diamonds, with arms raised upwards in a praying position.
Policoro (prov. of Matera). National Archaeological Museum of Siritide. Inv. 215924.
Bibliography: BIANCO 2012B, pg. 245.

28. 7. *Thymiaterion*
Matt-painted pottery. Beige-pink purified clay. Wheel-thrown vase.
Reassembled. Some parts missing on the rim/lip of the Ionic type cup and on the foot.
H 42.2 cm; rim: diam. 13.3 cm; foot: diam. 22.2 cm.
Tall, moulded body tapering towards the top; the top features an imitation Ionic cup; wide foot with a convex profile.
Two-tone painted decoration in black and red-brown; engraved decoration. On the Ionic cup, there are opposing bands and semicircles; on the trunk, there are alternating black and reddish-brown bands, and the mouldings feature engraved herringbone motifs.
Policoro (prov. of Matera). National Archaeological Museum of Siritide. Inv. 215901.
Bibliography: BIANCO 2012B, pg. 243.

28. 8. Twin vase
Matt-painted pottery. Refined beige-pink clay. Wheel-thrown vase.
Reassembled. Some parts missing on the rim/lip; decoration partly worn away.
H (with handle): 16.2 cm; length 27.8 cm; width 14.5 cm; single vase: h 10.5 cm, diam. 13 cm.
Twin vase consisting of two vases with a slightly flared body, rounded rim and straight lip. The two vases are connected by a single flat base that creates a perimeter recess on the outside and by a vertical handle with a circular shape, positioned at the point where the mouths of the two vases meet.
Two-tone painted decoration in black and red-brown. Small lines adorn the rim, while the body features diamonds filled with a grid pattern. Handle coloured in reddish-brown.
Policoro (prov. of Matera). National Archaeological Museum of Siritide. Inv. 215902.
Bibliography: BIANCO 2012B, pg. 243.

28. 9. Casket on anthropomorphic feet
Matt-painted pottery. Purified beige-pink clay. Hand-moulded container.
Reassembled with some parts missing; painted decoration largely worn away.
H (with bull protomes) 24 cm; length 24 cm; width 17.5 cm.
Rectangular casket with a double-pitched roof, set on four anthropomorphic feet. The various parts of the casket (walls and base) and the cover seem to have been made separately and then assembled together. The various connection points are accentuated with plastic strips, which have double-pointed appendages at the ends facing outwards. On the long sides of the cover, there are two central openings, one quad-

rangular and one rectangular, for the interlocking insertion of the hatch, which features a central hole and two smaller lateral holes.
Two-tone painted decoration in black and reddish-brown; includes plastic decoration. Casket, on the long walls: elongated diamond motifs; on short walls: meander motifs. In the tympanums, painted red, the spaces are delimited at the base by a flat strip and divided by a vertical strip painted in black with an oblique line pattern and a central segment. Double slope: vertical black bands, also found on one hatch. Ridge line, centre: two figures ornithomorphic plastics with same orientation; on the four extremities: opposite bull protomes painted in black on one side and in red on the other. The supports, painted in black, are shaped like anthropomorphic feet facing outwards on the long sides.
Policoro (prov. of Matera). National Archaeological Museum of Siritide. Inv. 215914.
Bibliography: BIANCO 2012B, pgs. 240-241.

The earthenware caskets are rare matt-painted ceramic artefacts found in some wealthy female tombs of the Enotro-Italic necropolis of San Vito (Guardia Perticara, prov. of Potenza), dating back to the 6th century BC. There are twelve known casket sets (BIANCO 2012B, pgs. 205-264). Three pieces were initially part of the Amati Collection of Potenza (BRUNN 1858, pgs. 159-168; BIANCO 2005B, pg. 396). This collection was broken up in the second half of the nineteenth century, and the artefacts were sold on the antiques market. Two of the three pieces are currently preserved: one at the *National Museum of Denmark* (Copenhagen), purchased at auction in 1891 and recorded as coming from Etruria, one at the *Musée du Louvre*, purchased on the antiques market in Naples and registered as coming from southern Italy (BIANCO 2005B, pg. 396; BIANCO 2012B, pgs. 207-209; BURANELLI 1985, pgs. 71-77; DAMGAARD ANDRSEN, WINGE HORSNÆNS 2002, pgs. 101-126); the third piece is lost. A sporadic piece from the necropolis area, initially kept in the Sacristy of the Mother Church of Guardia Perticara, was acquired by the Superintendency for Archaeological Heritage of Basilicata in 1996 (BIANCO 2012B, pgs. 216, 217). Eight pieces, uncovered during excavations conducted by the Superintendency between 1997 and 2007, come from tombs 122, 502, and 583 (displayed in the exhibition), 157, 259, 435, 619 and 631 (BIANCO 2012B, pgs. 217-260).
The caskets are formally similar. The only exception is the piece from tomb 502, which, unlike the others with a simple double-pitched roof, features a top part with a double slope. Such artefacts, in terms of form, find their closest parallels in contexts from central Italy, specifically in the Etruscan and Campania areas (BIANCO 2012B, pgs. 205-264; with previous bibliography).
The earthenware caskets are connected to the female sphere. The presence of the rectangular opening with a hatch on one of the two slopes suggests that it could be a miniature reproduction of chests that held a woman's goods. They were probably meant to hold and protect small cosmetic tools and precious personal ornaments.

29. Guardia Perticara (prov. of Potenza), San Vito area. Tomb 122
First half of the 6th century B.C
Shaft tomb (length 2.10 m; width 0.75 m), oriented NE-SW, bordered by large pebbles.

Inhumation burial of an adult female individual, placed in a supine position, with the skull facing west.
Excavations: Superintendency for Archaeological Heritage of Basilicata, year 1997.
Bibliography: BIANCO 2012B, pgs. 217-220.

Selected grave good
29. 1. Casket on anthropomorphic feet (fig. 19)
First half of the 6th century B.C
Matt-painted pottery. Beige-pink purified clay. Hand-moulded container. Reassembled with some parts missing; hatch on the slope missing; painted decoration largely worn away.
H 18.5 cm; length 18 cm; width 8.2 cm.
A casket shaped like a rectangular box with a double-pitched roof, standing on four anthropomorphic feet. The casket is not a single piece; it is composed of different parts (walls and base) and a cover that are assembled by interlocking.
Two-tone painted decoration in black and red, with additional plastic and engraved decorations. Casket, on the long walls: two-tone corner motifs with bands filled with hatching; on the short walls, two-tone square motifs. Double slope: reddish-brown squares bordered by a black band. On the ridge line: two plastic ornithomorphic applications, set on serpents coiled in spirals with engraved eyes and mouths. The supports, painted in black, are shaped like anthropomorphic feet facing outwards on the long sides.
Policoro (prov. of Matera). National Archaeological Museum of Siritide. Inv. 214855.
Bibliography: BIANCO 2012B, pgs. 217-219.

30. Guardia Perticara (prov. of Potenza), San Vito area. Tomb 583
First half of the 6th century B.C
Shaft tomb (length 3.23 m; width 1.10 m), oriented NS. The structure, located under tomb 581, was devoid of lithic covering and delimitation elements.
Inhumation burial of an adult female individual, placed in a supine position, with an S-shaped skull.
Excavations: Superintendency for Archaeological Heritage of Basilicata, year 2006.
Bibliography: BIANCO 2012B, pgs. 247-253.

Selected grave good
30. 1. Casket on anthropomorphic feet (fig. 20)
First half of the 6th century B.C
Matt-painted pottery. Purified beige-pink clay. Hand-moulded container. Not intact: painted decoration worn in parts.
H max 23.5 cm; length 26 cm; width 13.3 cm; hatch: width 6.4 cm, length 6.3 cm.
A casket shaped like a rectangular box with a double-pitched roof, standing on four anthropomorphic feet.
The various parts of the casket (walls and base) and the cover seem to have been made separately and then assembled together. The various connection points are accentuated with plastic strips, which have double-pointed appendages at the ends facing outwards. At the centre of a slope is a quadrangular opening for inserting the shaped hatch, which is equipped with a socket in the form of an ornithomorphic protome. On one side of the hatch are two holes, which are also present on the side wall of the slope, for the in-

19.

20.

sertion of filament-like elements (hinges). On the ridge line of the double slope, in the centre, there is a semi-circular handle.
Two-tone painted decoration in black and reddish-brown; includes plastic decoration. Casket, on the long walls: rhomboid motifs filled with elongated oval shapes featuring a dotted longitudinal band (possibly representing anthropomorphic figures or symbols of the female sphere), with intermediate triangular spaces filled in reddish-brown; on the short walls, similar semi-rhomboid motifs arranged horizontally. Double slope: St. Andrew's cross motifs bordered by dotted bands, with oval motifs at the ends. On the hatch: a vertical band featuring angular motifs and inscribed squares.
Plastic figures of ornithomimus, facing outwards, are positioned at the ends of the ridge line (only one of which is preserved) and at the corner vertices of the box. The supports, painted in black, are shaped like anthropomorphic feet facing outwards on the long sides; they still show the fingerprints from hand modelling.
Policoro (prov. of Matera). National Archaeological Museum of Siritide. Inv. 212360.
Bibliography: BIANCO 2012B, pg. 249.

31. Aliano-Alianello (prov. of Matera), Cazzaiola area. Tomb 309 (Cf. *supra*, pg. 39, fig. 10)

Late 8th - early 7th century BC
Rectangular shaft tomb (length 2.85 m; width 1.15 m), oriented EW.
Inhumation burial of an adult female individual, placed in a supine position, with the skull facing west.
Excavations: Archaeological Superintendency of Basilicata, year 1984.
Bibliography: BIANCO ET AL. 1996, pgs. 155-157.

Selected grave good
31. 1. Pyx on wheels with tesserae
Late 8th - early 7th century BC
Achromatic pottery. Purified beige-pink clay. Wheel-thrown pyx; hand-modelled tesserae.
Reassembled and incomplete (pyx); intact (tesserae).
Pyx on wheels: h. 11.8 cm; pyx: h. 7.1 cm; rim: diam. 5.7 cm; body: max diam. 9.5 cm, thick. 0.3 cm; base: diam. 6.1 cm; wheels: diam. 4.7 cm.
Lid: h 2.5 cm; max diam. 5.6 cm; handle: diam. 1.4 cm, thick. 1 cm.
Triangular tesserae: length 3 cm, width 3 cm; circular tesserae: diam. 3 cm.
Pyx with a globular body, featuring two oblique ribbon-shaped handles set on the upper part of the shoulder; rounded base with two protuberances at the front and back, each with a horizontal hole for inserting the axle of the four wheels, which are designed as circles with four trapezoidal spokes and have a rectangular section.
Hemispherical cap lid with two oblique ribbon-shaped handles positioned on the lower part of the cap and a cylindrical handle knob with an irregularly expanded top.
Twenty-eight triangular shaped tesserae (no. 14) and circular shaped tesserae (no. 14) each with three through holes. These tesserae would document a type of weaving, performed on a tablet, used for producing small bands of fabric such as belts, ribbons, borders, and more (CAPUTO, CERZOSO 2024, pg. 85). This refers to one of the most important productive activities associated with the female sphere in antiquity: weaving. Through this skill, along with the possession and management of other goods, the Oenotrian woman could achieve a high social status recognised by the community (BIANCO 2020, pgs. 99, 101; fig. 5).

Policoro (prov. of Matera). National Archaeological Museum of Siritide. Inv. 208338 (pyx), invv. 208345-208372 (tesserae).
Bibliography: Bianco et al. 1996, pg. 83, fig. below; Bottini 2000, pgs. 273-279; Nava et al. 2008, pgs. 288, 301, fig. 21, type AXXXVII S 2.1 (lid), type A XVII B 1.1 (pyx); Martelli 2012, pgs. 333, 334, figs. 27-29. Cf. triangular tesserae: Ferrante 2022, pg. 274, fig. 8.

Pisticci (MT), Incoronata area. Settlement
32. 1. *Deinos* with Bellerophon and Chimera, hourglass support (Cf. *supra*, pg. 19, fig. 2)

Second half/last quarter of the 7th century BC
Pottery. Orange-pink purified clay. Wheel-thrown vase and support.
Very thin, light beige-yellow engobe.
Reassembled and integrated. Parts missing on the bowl of *deinos* and on the lower base of the support; superficial abrasions of the colour.
Deinos with support: h 54.5 cm. *Deinos*: h 22 cm; rim: diam. 26.7 cm; lip: width 3.4 cm; body: max diam. 40 cm. Support: h 35.5 cm; upper base (chalice): diam. 20.5 cm; lower base: diam. 28 cm.
Deinos: globular-flattened body. Flat rim, oblique on the outside; rounded base (apode). Plastic ring handles with reel handles, positioned under the lip and attached to the shoulder; the reel is secured to the body of the vessel by a smooth cord located beneath the lip.
External surface. Decoration painted in brown, with a reddish hue, featuring geometric, phytomorphic, and zoomorphic motifs. On the rim/lip: a motif featuring two thin, spaced lines with a continuous double broken meander pattern in between. At the lip/shoulder junction: wide horizontal band. On the body, side A: a mythological scene depicting Bellerophon riding Pegasus (left) in battle against the Chimera (right); side B: a scene with two lions facing each other, standing and attacking a fawn (in the centre). In both decorative schemes, the main figures are accompanied by geometric and phytomorphic motifs. On both sides, the decorative patterns are bordered near the handles by a "sail" motif, outlined by two sets of three vertical segments that are parallel and closely spaced. The lower part of the *deinos* is filled and delimited above by four thin, horizontal and parallel lines. The handles are filled with colour.
Decoration engraved with thin lines, applied over the colour, to emphasize the locks of Pegasus's mane and to delineate the upper part of the horses' front legs.
Internal surface. Coloured background.
Support: hourglass body. The chalice and foot are truncated cone-shaped and are joined, at two-thirds of the total height, by a spherical-flattened bulge bordered by two thin, smooth cords. The chalice has a triple convex profile rim.
Monochrome painted decoration in brown, with a reddish hue, featuring geometric motifs composed of bands, lines, segments, vertically juxtaposed corners, and zigzags.
Origin: Saggio S, Greek *oikos* nr. 12. The Greek *oikos* has been reinterpreted by Mario Denti (2024, pgs. 35, 37 and chap. 5) as a "ritual deposit".
Excavations: University of Milan, year 1986.
Bernalda-Metaponto (prov. of Matera). National Archaeological Museum of Metaponto. Inv. 298978 (*deinos*), inv. 298979 (support).
Bibliography: Orlandini 1986, pgs. 689-691 Orlandini 1987, pgs. 688-690, plates XCVI, XCVII; Orlandini 1988, pgs. 6-16; Orlandini 1995, pg. 57, figs. 175-178; De Siena 2002, pgs. 36-38; Colucci 2002, pg. 143, nr. 1; Denti 2024, pgs. 43-46, nr. 3 in catalogue (with previous bibliography).
Attribution: Pittore dei Cavalli (Denti 2024, pgs. 250-262, 321).

Pisticci (MT), Incoronata area. Settlement
32. 2. *Deinos* with horses, tripod and tree of life (Cf. *supra*, pg. 19, fig. 1)
Second half/last quarter of the 7th century BC
Pottery. Orange-pink purified clay. Wheel-thrown vase.
Very thin engobe, light beige-yellow in colour; in the areas inside the handles, without engobe, traces of the splints are visible.
Reassembled about halfway; surfaces chipped and abraded in places.
H 27.5 cm; rim, length of rope: 26.5 cm; lip: width 4.5 cm; body: max diam. 41.5 cm, wall thick. 0.75 cm.
Globular-flattened body. Flat rim, slightly oblique on the outside; rounded base (apode). Plastic ring handles with reel handles, positioned under the lip and attached to the shoulder; the reel is secured to the body of the vessel by a smooth cord located beneath the lip.
External surface. Decoration painted in dark brown, with a reddish hue in poorly fired areas, featuring geometric, phytomorphic, and zoomorphic motifs. On the rim/lip: a motif consisting of two sets of thin, closely spaced lines, with the space between them filled by a continuous triple spiral and single dots. At the lip/shoulder junction: wide band and thin line, horizontal and parallel. On the body, side A: two standing horses facing each other in profile, with a large tripod in the centre; side B: two standing horses facing each other in profile, with a "tree of life" motif in the centre. In both decorative schemes, the main figures are accompanied by geometric and phytomorphic motifs. On both sides the decorative patterns are closed near the handles by a "sail" motif bordered by two series of four vertical segments, parallel and close together. The lower part of the *deinos* is filled and delimited above by four thin, horizontal and parallel lines. The handles are filled with colour.
Internal surface. Coloured background with unglazed bottom.
Origin: Saggio T, Greek *oikos* nr. 13. The Greek *oikos* has been reinterpreted by MARIO DENTI (2024, pgs. 35, 43 and chap. 5) as a "ritual deposit".
Excavations: University of Milan, year 1988.
Bernalda-Metaponto (prov. of Matera). National Archaeological Museum of Metaponto. Inv. 299759.
Bibliography: ORLANDINI 1991, pgs. 1, 2, 5-7, figs. 10, 11, plate II; ORLANDINI 1992, pg. 71, no. 2, figs. 125, 126, 185-187; DENTI 2024, pgs. 37-40, nr. 1 in catalogue (with previous bibliography).
Attribution: Pittore dei Cavalli (DENTI 2024, pgs. 250-262, 322).

Pisticci (MT), Incoronata area. Settlement.
32. 3. *Stamnos* with lion (Cf. *supra*, pg. 42, fig. 12)
Mid/second quarter of the 7th century BC
Pottery. Beige-pink purified clay. Wheel-thrown vase.
Reassembled and largely intact.
H 38 cm; rim: diam. 21 cm; body: max diam. 45 cm.
Globular body. Flat rim; short, collared lip; low, truncated conical foot; vertical, slightly oblique, ribbon-shaped handles with an elliptical section, set on the shoulder.
Decoration painted in brown, with a reddish hue, featuring geometric, phytomorphic, and zoomorphic motifs. The rim, lip, upper shoulder, lower body and foot are filled with colour. On the shoulder: a motif consisting of ten thin, horizontal, parallel lines with a central chessboard pattern created by adding oblique segments; this motif borders the decorative metope scheme at the top. On the body, side A: in the centre, a metope with a crouching, roaring lion facing right, with a long tail raised and bent in an S-shape, left unglazed; above the lion's back is a large, stylised eight-petalled rosette, filled in, with an unglazed *corolla* and a filled central point.

Side B: in the centre, metope with two opposing vertical spirals, rendered with a double line, with upper spirals closed on the inside and the lower ones open on the outside. The two spirals are joined at the top and base by two series of horizontal, parallel segments, from which hanging palmette motifs and petal motifs filled with colour emerge.

On both sides (A-B), the central metopes are outlined by a geometric decorative pattern consisting of two scalene triangles filled with colour, rotated 90° and joined at the vertex to create an unglazed hourglass shape. This motif is defined on the outer side (near the handles) by a series of ten closely spaced vertical segments, extending up to the upper part of the shoulder. On the inner side (next to the central metope), it is bordered by a series of eight or nine closely spaced vertical and parallel segments, accompanied by a sinuous vertical band filled with colour.

The metope scheme is closed at the base by a motif of eight thin, horizontal and parallel lines. On the lower part of the body: a motif of large spokes filled with colour and outlined by a thin line; the motif concludes at the base with a series of horizontal bands that connect to the background.

The handles, filled with colour on the external surface, are set within an unglazed frame. In the lower half, there is a motif of ten thin, horizontal, parallel lines with a central chessboard pattern.

Origin: Saggio T, Greek *oikos* nr. 13. The Greek *oikos* has been reinterpreted by MARIO DENTI (2024, pgs. 35, 79 and chap. 5) as a "ritual deposit".

Excavations: University of Milan, 1988.

Bernalda-Metaponto (prov. of Matera). National Archaeological Museum of Metaponto. Inv. 299739.

Bibliography: ORLANDINI 1991, pgs. 2, 3, plate 1; ORLANDINI 1992, pg. 71, figs. 183, 184; CRACOLICI, D'ONGHIA 2023, pg. 28; DENTI 2024, pgs. 78, 79, nr. 30 in catalogue (with previous bibliography).

Attribution: Pittore dei Leoni (DENTI 2024, pgs. 262-271, 322).

Pisticci (MT), Incoronata area. Settlement.
32. 4. *Aryballos* with Griffins (Cf. *supra*, pg. 20, fig. 3)
Second half/late phase 7th century BC
Pottery. Orange purified clay. Wheel-thrown vase.
Very thin, light-yellow engobe.
Reassembled and largely intact.
H 28,5 cm; rim: diam. 14.5 cm; body: max diam. 27 cm.
Ovoid body with slightly tapered lower part. Slanting rim on the inside; large, strongly curved lip, cylindrical in shape with a convex profile; short cylindrical neck; low, truncated conical foot.

External surface. Decoration painted in dark brown; beige is used for the necks of the griffins and parts of the phytomorphic motifs; part of the vase has a red-orange decoration caused by oxidation from excessive firing. The decorative scheme consists of geometric, phytomorphic, and zoomorphic motifs.

The rim, neck, upper shoulder and lower body are filled with colour. On the lip: checkerboard pattern. On the upper part of the body: decoration arranged in two metope sections, separated by a vertical motif of five or six inscribed squares bordered by a double line; within the two metopes, there are phytomorphic and zoomorphic motifs, mythological beings, and human figures. The longest metope depicts a scene with two lions at the ends, leaning back with some paws resting on stylized phytomorphic motifs. In the centre are two crouching Griffins in a heraldic position, placed on either side of a scroll and palmette motif. On one side, between a Griffin and a lion, is a stylized male figure in profile (with only the torso shown frontally), moving to the right, holding a spear in his right hand

and with his left arm extended forward. Between the human figure and the leaning lion is a large bird facing left, toward the human figure.
The shorter metope depicts a complex phytomorphic interweaving made up of spirals and palmettes.
The metope decorative scheme is defined at the top by a motif of four horizontal, parallel lines and at the base by a motif consisting of two spaced sets of four horizontal, parallel lines, with the space in between filled by a broken meander pattern.
Decoration engraved with thin lines to highlight figures and phytomorphic motifs.
Unglazed foot.
Internal surface. Light brown background.
Origin: Saggio S, Greek *oikos* nr. 12. The Greek *oikos* has been reinterpreted by MARIO DENTI (2024, pgs. 35, 127 and chap. 5) as a "ritual deposit".
Excavations: University of Milan, year 1986.
Bernalda-Metaponto (prov. of Matera). National Archaeological Museum of Metaponto. Inv. 298980.
Bibliography: ORLANDINI 1986, pgs. 689-691; ORLANDINI 1987, pgs. 688-690, plate XCVIII; ORLANDINI 1995, pg. 57, figs. 179-182; DE FAVERI 2005, pg. 390; DENTI 2024, pgs. 127-131, nr. 71 in the catalogue (with previous bibliography).
Attribution: Pittore dei Grifi (DENTI 2024, pgs. 271-279, 321)

33. Bernalda-Metaponto (MT), Crucinia area, Giacovelli property. Tomb 566 (Cf. *supra*, pg. 42, fig. 13)

Early 6th century BC
Semi-chamber tomb (interior: length 2.45 m; width 1.45 m; depth 1.25 m) made up of nine square blocks of *carparo* stone, of different shapes and sizes, oriented NW-SE. Two blocks, one with a lateral recess for interlocking and one shaped, suggest a probable reuse. The two roof slabs, found broken and fallen inside, perhaps the result of a robbery, damaged the skeleton and the grave goods. The base of the structure was made of irregular slabs.
Inhumation burial of an adult male (over 60 years of age), placed in a supine position, with the skull facing SE.
Excavations: Superintendency for Archaeological Heritage of Basilicata, year 1992.
Bibliography: BOTTINI 1993, pg. 708; BOTTINI *ET AL.* 2019, pgs. 64-70.

Selected grave goods
33. 1. Corinthian *Alabastron*
Pottery. Beige purified clay. Wheel-thrown vase.
Reassembled; painted decoration largely faded and worn away.
H 11.2 cm; rim: diam. 3.3 cm; lip: thick. 0.4 cm; body: max diam. 6 cm; base: diam. 5.5 cm; handle: 0.6 cm.
Ovoid body. Flat rim; discoid lip; short, concave neck; slightly convex base; small vertical perforated handle with an elliptical section, extending from the rim/lip to the base of the neck.
Two-tone painted decoration (black, red-brown) with geometric, phytomorphic and zoomorphic motifs. On the rim and lip: a series of radial tongues; on the body: two panthers facing each other, with bodies in profile, crouched on their hind legs, muzzles facing forward, and tails raised and curved. The scene is surrounded by rosette motifs, with splashes of colour, with graffiti segments combined in a simple or multiple cross. Base: radial petal motif.
Bernalda-Metaponto (prov. of Matera). National Archaeological Museum of Metaponto. Inv. 321378.

Bibliography: Bottini *ET AL.* 2019, pgs. 65, 108, figs. 6, 76, plate II. 1, 2, no. 1 in the catalogue.

33. 2. Laconic *Aryballos*
Pottery. Orange purified clay. Wheel-thrown vase.
Reassembled, abraded surface; painted decoration slightly faded.
H 7.3 cm; rim: diam. 4.8 cm; lip: thick. 0.25 cm; body: max diam. 7.5 cm; base: diam. 2 cm.
Globular-flattened body. Thin, rounded rim; discoid lip; short cylindrical neck; omphalos; vertical ribbon-shaped handle set from rim/lip to shoulder.
Two-tone painted decoration (dark grey degraded into reddish brown, shiny red) with horizontal band motif. Rim, lip, neck, body and handle: dark grey background; on the body, above the maximum expansion: broad red band bordered by two thin unglazed bands.
Bernalda-Metaponto (prov. of Matera). National Archaeological Museum of Metaponto. Inv. 321388.
Bibliography: Bottini *ET AL.* 2019, pgs. 65, 66, 107, figs. 6, 74, nr. 2 in catalogue.

33. 3. Pyx
Achromatic pottery. Dark grey purified clay. Wheel-thrown vase.
Reassembled; chipping on the rim; encrustations on the surface.
H 6.45 cm; rim: diam. 6.25 cm; lip: thick. 0.7 cm; body: max diam. 9 cm; base: diam. 3.85 cm.
Biconical body. Flat rim; slightly flared and shaped lip on the outside; slightly concave base.
Plastic decoration. On the shoulder: two parallel horizontal grooves.
Bernalda-Metaponto (prov. of Matera). National Archaeological Museum of Metaponto. Inv. 321389.
Bibliography: Bottini *ET AL.* 2019, pg. 66, figs. 6, 79, no. 3 in the catalogue.

33. 4. Chiota chalice
Pottery. Beige purified clay, wheel-thrown. White engobe.
Reassembled and integrated; painted decoration partly worn away.
H 13.5 cm; rim: diam. 19 cm; lip: thick. 0.3/4 cm; keel: diam. 14.5 cm; foot: diam. 6.4 cm; handles: 1.1 cm x 1 cm.
Keeled body. Thinned rim; high, flared lip; shallow bowl with a rounded keel; hollow, truncated conical foot; horizontal handles with a circular section, positioned on the keel.
Monochrome external and internal decoration (glossy black, diluted and degraded to red) featuring geometric, phytomorphic, and ornithomorphic motifs.
External surface: *"on the rim a row of black rectangles alternating with unglazed rectangles with a central dot. Above the handles, there is a quadripartite area created by a double-crossed line, filled with four triangles converging toward the centre. Each triangle is divided into three, forming a central diamond and two lateral triangles. On each side, arranged vertically, is a sequence of unglazed rectangles with a central point, framed by two bands. On the wall, at the level of the handles, there is an unglazed band decorated with rosettes surrounded by a circle of dots, framed above by inverted triangles and below by a painted band. Below that is a continuous meander, bordered beneath by a painted band. At the base, there is a spoke motif, and the foot is painted with an achromatic background. Side A: on the lip four geese moving to the right; eye, beak and some body parts unglazed. Fillers: pendants (triangles, discs); in the field, swastikas with tips, diamonds, and rosettes with a circle of dots."* (Bottini *ET AL.* 2019, pg. 66). Side B: decoration difficult to read.

Inner surface: background with unglazed band on the rim.
Bernalda-Metaponto (prov. of Matera). National Archaeological Museum of Metaponto. Inv. 321425.
Bibliography: BOTTINI ET AL. 2019, pgs. 66, 119, 122, 160, 161, figs. 6, 82, plate III. 1-3, no. 4 in the catalogue.

33. 5. Trilobate *oinochoe*
Laminated bronze, cast handle and cylinder; silver.
Reassembled and incomplete.
H (with handle) 30.2 cm; rim: length 12 cm, width 11.5 cm; lip: thick. 0.45/0.5; body: max diam. 19 cm, thick. 0.2 cm; handle: width 3.5 cm, thick. 0.65 cm.
Globular-flattened body. Oblique rim on the outside; flared trilobate lip; high, concave neck; very low, slightly convex foot, formed from the same lamina as the bowl. Vertical ribbon-shaped handle shaped with three longitudinal ribs, set from under the lip to the maximum expansion of the body. At the top, the ribbon is attached to the lip by three pins, each topped with a large head covered in silver lamina on the inside of the mouthpiece. The two side pins go all the way through and have heads on the opposite ends as well, while the third, central pin is purely decorative, shorter, and does not protrude. At the base, the ribbon, which ends with a moulded cylinder, is probably fixed with an adhesive.
Decoration engraved with thin horizontal lines, organised in two spaced bands, placed on the shoulder.
Bernalda-Metaponto (prov. of Matera). National Archaeological Museum of Metaponto. Inv. 321374, 321379.
Bibliography: BOTTINI ET AL. 2019, pgs. 68, 129, 130, fig. 85, plate IV. 1, 2, no. 5 in the catalogue.

33. 6. *Phiale*
Silver plated.
Reassembled and very incomplete.
H (reconstructed) 3.4 cm; rim: diam. 15.5 cm; lip: thick. 0.15 cm.
Flat rim; flared lip; shallow spherical bowl; flat base.
Embossed decoration on the base consisting of a sixteen-petalled corolla.
Bernalda-Metaponto (prov. of Matera). National Archaeological Museum of Metaponto. Inv. 321375.
Bibliography: BOTTINI ET AL. 2019, pgs. 68, 135, 136, figs. 7, 88, nr. 6 in the catalogue.

33. 7. Grip-tongue sword
Wrought iron, bronze, ivory, silver, gold.
Reassembled and partially incomplete.
Total length (reconstruction) 90 cm; blade: max. width 4 cm, min. width 2.6 cm, thick. 1.1 cm; hilt: length 7.4 cm, max. width 3.65 cm, thick. 1.6 cm; termination: h 3 cm, residual width 5 cm; iron cap: diam. 2.3 cm; bronze terminal cap: diam. 2 cm.
Long, narrow iron blade with bilateral cut and longitudinal median rib with deep lateral grooves. Grip-tongue hilt with a slightly diamond-shaped profile and subtly raised edges designed to hold the ivory heels, secured with an iron nail. The end features a truncated cone-shaped ivory core, topped by two small caps - the first made of iron and the second of bronze. The bronze cap is covered with two thin, overlapping sheets: the first in silver and the second in gold, all fastened with an iron pin.
Of the scabbard, not preserved, in perishable material, perhaps leather, part of an ivory plaque with a curved profile remains, perhaps relating to the tip.
Bernalda-Metaponto (prov. of Matera). National Archaeological Museum of Metaponto. Inv. 321387, 321406, 321421.

Bibliography: BOTTINI ET AL. 2019, pgs. 68, 139, 140, figs. 8, 9, plate VII. 1, nr. 7 in the catalogue. This piece is classified as: Iron grip-tongue swords: a) type without handguard (BOTTINI ET AL. 2019). The authors (p. 139) classify the piece as Snodgrass Type 1 (SNODGRASS 1964).

33. 8. Spherical head nails
Bronze, silver plating, gold.
Intact.
Sphere: diam. 2,3 cm, thick. 0,05 cm; stems: 0,22 cm x 0,2 cm.
Stem in bronze bar, with irregular quadrangular section; dome-shaped head with internal, central hollow, into which the stem is inserted.
Bernalda-Metaponto (prov. of Matera). National Archaeological Museum of Metaponto. Inv. 321407, 321411_A.
Bibliography: BOTTINI ET AL. 2019, pgs. 68, 150, plate VIII. 8A, no. 8A in catalogue.

33. 9. Pin end
Wrought iron, bronze, gold.
1) ends: length 11.65 cm; stem: diam. 0.85 cm; head/cap: diam. 2.3 cm.
2) ends: length 6.6 cm; stem: diam. 0.85 cm; head/cap: diam. 2.3 cm.
Stem in iron bar, with a circular section, with one end closed by a bronze cap covered with gold leaf (thick. 0.05 cm). The bar (stem) is flanked by two long, thin bronze bars, with a circular section; the whole, covered in ivory on the upper part, is inserted into the wood of which traces also remain along the stems.
The two elements could constitute the ends of a single pin, pertaining to the central axis that connected the two pairs of legs of a *diphros* (Bottini *et al.* 2019, pg. 149).
Bernalda-Metaponto (prov. of Matera). National Archaeological Museum of Metaponto. Inv. 321394, 321401.
Bibliography: BOTTINI ET AL. 2019, pgs. 69, 149, plate VIII. 3, 11, no. 11 in catalogue.

33. 10. End elements of table or stool legs
Laminated bronze, wood.
1) piece with wood residues inside: length 14 cm, width 2.9 cm, lamina thickness 0.15 cm.
2) piece: length 15 cm; width 4.3 cm, lamina thickness 0.15 cm.
3) piece: length 14.2 cm, width 3.65 cm, thickness 0.15 cm.
Intact.
Three artfacts with an arched profile, consisting of two pairs of shaped, slightly curved sheets arranged in a cross to form a cage, and connected by nails. Inside one piece, wood residues are preserved.
Bernalda-Metaponto (prov. of Matera). National Archaeological Museum of Metaponto. Inv. 321376, 321390, 321391.
Bibliography: BOTTINI ET AL. 2019, pgs. 69, 149, 150, figs. 10, 96, nr. 12 in the catalogue.

34. Bernalda-Metaponto (MT), Crucinia area, Giacovelli property. Tomb 610 (Cf. *supra*, pgs. 42-43, figs. 13-14)
First half of the 6th century BC
Semi-chamber tomb (interior dimensions: length 2.2 m; width 1.35 m; depth 1.35 m) made of squared blocks of *carparo*, showing the joint lines and clamp housings, oriented NW-SE. The walls are made of fifteen blocks of different shapes and sizes. The roof is made up of three blocks, supported on the short south-east side by stone fragments. The base is made up

of nine blocks of various shapes and sizes. The housings for the clamps indicate the probable connection of five wall blocks on the upper plane.
Inhumation burial of an adult male (50/60 years of age), poorly preserved, placed in a supine position, with the skull facing SE.
Excavations: Superintendency for Archaeological Heritage of Basilicata, year 1993.
Bibliography: BOTTINI 1993, pg. 708; BOTTINI ET AL. 2019, pgs. 70-76.

Selected grave goods
34. 1. Pyx
Achromatic pottery. Orange-pink purified clay. Wheel-thrown vase.
Incomplete rim/lip and the bowl.
H 8.55 cm; rim: 8.3 cm; lip: width 1.15 cm, thick. 0.4 cm; body: max diam. 13.5 cm; base: diam. 4.8 cm.
Globular-flattened body. Slanted rim on the inside; short flared lip; indistinct, slightly convex base.
Plastic and engraved decoration. At the lip/shoulder junction, there is a thin horizontal plastic moulding with a straight profile. On the shoulder, three horizontal engraved lines are present: the two upper lines are close together, while the lower one is spaced apart, creating two rounded mouldings.
Bernalda-Metaponto (prov. of Matera). National Archaeological Museum of Metaponto. Inv. 321883.
Bibliography: BOTTINI ET AL. 2019, pgs. 70, 117, 129, 391, figs. 14, 79, no. 2 in the catalogue.

34. 2. *Alabastron*
Alabaster.
Intact.
H 31 cm; rim: diam. 2.55 cm; body: max diam. 3.2 cm; base: diam. 1.05 cm.
Elongated body. Slanted rim on the outside; flared lip and neck; irregularly flat base. Two small vertical semi-circular handles are present on the upper part of the body.
Bernalda-Metaponto (prov. of Matera). National Archaeological Museum of Metaponto. Inv. 321884.
Bibliography: BOTTINI ET AL. 2019, pgs. 70, 73, 129, 321, figs. 14, 84, no. 3 in the catalogue.

34. 3. Trilobate "Rhodian" *oinochoe*
Bronze, probably cast in all major parts.
Restored; parts missing on the handle.
H 34 cm; rim: length 14 cm, width 13.5 cm; lip: thick. 0.8 cm; neck: diam. 8.15 cm; body: max diam. 19.5 cm; foot: diam. 8.5 cm; handle: width 3.55 cm, thick. 1.55 cm.
Pear-shaped body. Thickened rim with an oblique outer profile; flared lip; cylindrical neck; hollow, truncated cone-shaped foot with a hollow upper section that accommodates the lower part of the body. Vertical ribbon-shaped handle, set from the rim/lip to the shoulder, made up of several components. Ribbon: a sheet with edges folded outward, terminating in a polylobed plate, secured to the shoulder with two small nails. The sheet encases three small vertical tubes, visible from the outside, with a moulded cylinder attached to their base. The upper attachment of the ribbon, more complex in design, consists of a large cylindrical element with a disc-shaped end featuring a moulded edge, which is positioned on the rim/lip. At the base, this element terminates in a small plate: the internal surface of the lip has a polylobed profile, secured with two small nails, while the external surface has a smooth, semi-circular

profile. The vertical handle is set on the element with a disc-shaped end, to the base of which a moulded cylinder is fixed.
Plastic decoration placed halfway up the neck consisting of a moulding with a rounded profile.
Bernalda-Metaponto (prov. of Matera). National Archaeological Museum of Metaponto. Inv. 321879.
Bibliography: BOTTINI *ET AL*. 2019, pgs. 70, 73, 130-133, 139, 161, fig. 15, plates IV. 3, V. 1, nr. 4 in catalogue. The authors (p. 131) classify the piece as Type A (SHEFTON 1979; SHEFTON 2009).

34. 4. *Phiale mesonphalos*
Laminated silver and gold.
Damage and small parts missing especially on the gold plate.
H 3.5/85 cm, rim: diam. 20.5 cm, thick. 0.42 cm; gold disc: diam. 9.25 cm, thick. 0.08; *omphalos*: diam. 4.8 cm.
Flat rim, slightly thickened on the inside; short, straight-profile lip, slightly flared; deep bowl with a gently rounded profile. The base consists of a low annular ridge that separates the outermost part, which is slightly hollowed out, from the innermost part, which is taut and oblique. This inner section is covered with gold leaf, with a second gold leaf superimposed, limited to the *omphalos* only.
Embossed decoration with geometric, phytomorphic and zoomorphic motifs. On the bowl: an interlacing motif of thirty-three pairs of stylized lotus leaves, each split at the tip, creating deep radial pods that are shaped and concave in profile, with the wider end facing inward. The decoration concludes, just below the attachment of the lip, with a wolf's tooth motif.
Inside, on the gold lamina surrounding the *omphalos*: decoration arranged in two concentric bands. The first, more internal, features a double spiral motif arranged obliquely and separated by palmettes, facing alternately inwards and outwards. The second frieze features a series of eight figures of animals in motion, shown in profile, alternating with geometric and phytomorphic motifs (such as spirals, double spirals, and rosettes). In this register, there are only two pairs of facing animals: a bull and a lion, followed by two capercaillies. In both cases, at the point of contact phytomorphic motifs are inserted; on the sides, the remaining four zoomorphic figures: a panther, a donkey, a horse and a lion.
Bernalda-Metaponto (prov. of Matera). National Archaeological Museum of Metaponto. Inv. 321888.
Bibliography: BOTTINI *ET AL*. 2019, pgs. 70, 74, 136, 138, 139, 161, fig. 89, plate VI, no. 7 in the catalogue.

34. 5. Grip-tongue sword
Wrought iron, bronze, silver, wood.
Only two non-rejoinable parts remain; the median section is missing.
Residual length 42.5 cm; blade: width 3.1 cm, thick. 1.5 cm; hilt: length 9.4 cm, max width 2.7 cm, thick. 0.75 cm.
Long iron blade with bilateral cutting edge, lenticular section. Grip-tongue sword style hilt with a slightly contoured profile and short lateral fins; both are surrounded by folded bronze lamina, such as to hold the silver heels fixed with three iron nails.
On one silver heel is visible a motif engraved with dense oblique hatching. Of the wooden scabbard there remain some fragments present on the blade.

Bernalda-Metaponto (prov. of Matera). National Archaeological Museum of Metaponto. Inv. 321889.
Bibliography: BOTTINI ET AL. 2019, pgs. 70, 74, 140, 141, 161, fig. 19, plate VII. 2, no. 8 in the catalogue. This piece is classified as: Iron Grip-tongue sword swords: b) type with winglet-shaped handguards (BOTTINI *et al.* 2019).

34. 6. *Machaira*
Wrought iron, wood.
Reassembled and incomplete; missing the tip.
Length 51 cm; blade: max. width 5, min. width 3.5 cm, thick. 0.9 cm; hilt: length 12 cm, width 3 cm, width with apophysis 4.7 cm, thick. 0.85/0.9 cm; hand socket: width 8.95 cm.
Weapon with a single-edged blade featuring an elongated triangular section; an arched back with a flat upper profile; a sinuous cutting edge; the blade widens halfway along its length and likely maintains the same width up to the tip, which is missing. Hilt with a curved back, continuing the profile of the blade's spine, and an elongated triangular section; in the lower part, it has two short inward-bent apophysis that define the hand's position.
Traces of wood on the blade.
Bernalda-Metaponto (prov. of Matera). National Archaeological Museum of Metaponto. Inv. 321891.
Bibliography: BOTTINI ET AL. 2019, pgs. 70, 75, 142, 143, 386, figs. 20, 90, nr. 9 in catalogue. The authors (p. 142) include the piece in Type III Verchik (VERCHIK 2014, pg. 67, fig. 8).

34. 7. Grip-tongue knife
Wrought iron, wood.
Reassembled; minor parts missing.
Length 35.5 cm; blade: max. width 3.3, min. width 2.7 cm, thick. 0.6 cm; hilt: length 7 cm, width 2.65 cm, thick. 0.25.
Iron blade with an elongated triangular section; a slightly arched back with a flat upper profile; a slightly sinuous cut; the blade widens slightly in the terminal half and then narrows near the tip. Grip-tongue hilt, with an elongated rectangular section.
Traces of wood on the hilt.
Bernalda-Metaponto (prov. of Matera). National Archaeological Museum of Metaponto. Inv. 321892.
Bibliography: BOTTINI ET AL. 2019, pgs. 70, 75, 143; figs. 21, 91, no. 10 in catalogue.

34. 8. Grip-tongue knife
Forged iron.
Incomplete.
Length 20.5 cm; blade: max width 2.45 cm, min width 1.95 cm, thick. 0.2 cm; hilt: width 1.65 cm, thick. 0.3 cm.
Iron blade with an elongated triangular section; a slightly arched back with a flat upper profile; a sinuous cutting edge; the blade widens in the terminal half and then narrows towards the tip. Grip-tongue hilt, with an elongated rectangular section, the end is missing.
Bernalda-Metaponto (prov. of Matera). National Archaeological Museum of Metaponto. Inv. 321894.
Bibliography: BOTTINI ET AL. 2019, pgs. 70, 75, 143; figs. 21, 91, nr. 11 in catalogue.

34. 9. Pair of carriage pins
Cast bronze.
Intact.
Length 10.2 cm; discs: diam. 3.8 cm, thick. 0.6 cm; bar: length 6.95 cm., diam. 0.8 cm; cap h 0.9 cm, diam 1.7 cm.
Bar, with a circular section. One end terminates in a disc with a moulded profile, topped by a cap, while the other end is inserted into a similar disc, where the separate cap, featuring an annular groove, served as a fastening nut.
Bernalda-Metaponto (prov. of Matera). National Archaeological Museum of Metaponto. Inv. 321881, 321882.
Bibliography: BOTTINI *ET AL*. 2019, pgs. 70, 75, 151, 388; figs. 22, 97, no. 14 in catalogue.

Glossary

Alabastron	Alabaster flask with a narrow mouth, usually elongated, used to contain perfume
Andiron/s	Iron or bronze stands for supporting spits to cook meat
Anthropomorph	Figure with human form and attributes, at times stylised
Artemision	Temple of Artemis
Aryballos	Small flask with a narrow mouth used to contain perfume
Bracteate	Ornamental disc with a hemispherical cap and a pointed or smooth centre, with a slot or two holes for sewing it to ceremonial/funerary garments
Chalcophone	Musical instrument with resonators, worn as a pendant in high-status female burials
Ware pottery	Pottery, poorly purified, mostly hand-worked
Matt-painted pottery	Depurated pottery with matt-painted decoration, documented between the 9th and 5th centuries BC in southern Campania, Basilicata, northern Calabria and Apulia
Giant Triton Shell	*Charonia tritonis* (Linnaeus, 1758)
Deinos or *Dinos*	Large bowl with a narrow mouth used to contain wine
Diphros	Ancient stool with neither a backrest nor armrests
Enchytrismos	Infant burial inside a large jar
Etagenperücke	A horizontally layered coiffure
Ethnos, ethne	People, peoples
Phalera	Ornamental circular pendant with internal spokes, threaded and suspended on belts or other supports
Fibula	Brooch with a pin and a simple or composite arch, of various sizes, used to hold together parts of a veil/robe/cloak and as a ceremonial/funerary ornament
Phytomorph	Figure with the form and attributes of a plant, at times stylised
Genos	Family group, lineage
Heraion	Temple of Hera
Hydria	Large or medium-sized three-handled jar with a narrow mouth, used to carry water

Kalathos	Vase with a wide mouth, usually with a truncated cone shape, used to measure and contain solid foods and liquids
Kantharos	Cup with a narrow mouth, of various sizes, with two high vertical handles, used for drinking wine
Kotyle	Cup with a wide mouth and two horizontal handles, used for drinking
Makhaira or *Kopis*	Weapon, similar to a sword or large knife, with a single recurved blade
Oinochoe	Jug with a three-lobed mouth used for pouring wine
Olla	Very large jar with a narrow mouth used to contain and store solid foods and liquids
Olpe	Vessel similar to a jug, of various sizes, used for pouring wine
Omphalos	The raised boss (convex) in the centre of the bottom of a *phiale* (a bowl, similar to a cup)
Ornithomorph	Figure with the form and attributes of a bird/winged animal, at times stylised
Phiale	Bowl, similar to a cup, with an omphalos (convex), used in sacred ceremonies and rituals
Pyx	Box, sometimes with a lid, used to contain women's jewellery and toiletries
Polis/Poleis	City-State in Ancient Greece
Polos	Crown, of various shapes (spherical, cylindrical, quadrangular) and sizes, typically worn by a few female deities and women in cultic rituals
Protome	Figure of the head of a human, animal or fantastical being, sometimes with the upper torso
Pin	Pin with a simple or composite head, used to hold together parts of a veil/robe/cloak and as a ceremonial/funerary ornament
Stamnos	Large or medium-sized jar with a narrow mouth, usually with a globular body, used to contain wine
Synmachoi	Allies (in war)
Thymatherion	Medium-sized vase with a narrow mouth, usually cylindrical, used to burn incense
Xenia	Food given to guests and put in the rooms offered to them by the master of the household
Zoomorph	Figure with the form and attributes of an animal, at times stylised

Bibliography

Abulafia 2013 = D. Abulafia, *The Great Sea: A Human History of the Mediterranean*, It. trans. *Il grande mare. Storia del Mediterraneo*, Milan 2013.

Adamesteanu 1999 = D. Adamesteanu (ed.), *Storia della Basilicata - 1. L'Antichità*, in G. De Rosa, A. Cestaro (eds.), *Storia della Basilicata*, Rome-Bari, 1999.

Adamesteanu, Dilthey 1978 = D. Adamesteanu, H. Dilthey, *Siris. Nuovi contributi archeologici*, in *Mélanges de l'École française de Rome. Antiquités*, XC, 1978, pp. 515-565.

Affuso 2010 = A. Affuso, *Evidenze archeologiche pre-protostoriche nella valle dal Sauro (Basilicata)*, in *Studi per l'ecologia del Quaternario*, 32, 2010, pp. 21-29.

Affuso, Bianco 2011 = A. Affuso, S. Bianco, *Itinerari della transumanza nel medio bacino dell'Agri (Basilicata) dalla preistoria all'età moderna*, in F. Lugli, A. Stoppiello, S. Biagetti (eds.), Atti 4° Convegno Nazionale di Etnoarcheologia (Rome, 17 - 19 May 2006), *British Archaeological Reports. International Series* 2235, 2011, pp. 207-217.

Affuso et al. 2012 = A. Affuso, S. Bianco, P. Lorusso, A. Preite, *La plastica antropomorfa e zoomorfa nelle produzioni enotriojapigie tra bronzo finale e prima età del ferro*, in Atti XLII Riunione Scientifica dell'Istituto Italiano di Preistoria e Pro- tostoria (Trento, 9-13 October 2007), Trento 2012, pp. 353-358.

Anderson 2005 = G. Anderson, *Before Turannoi Were Tyrants: Rethinking a Chapter of Early Greek History*, in *Classical Antiquity*, 24 (2), 2005, pp. 173-222.

Antonaccio 2003 = C. M. Antonaccio, *Hybridity and cultures within Greek Culture*, C. Dougherty, L. Kurke (eds.), *The Cultures within Greek Culture: contact, conflict, collaboration*, Cambridge 2003, pp. 57-74.

Aurigny 2017 = H. Aurigny, *Greek art in the seventh century BC: the example of bronzes from Delphi*, in X. Charalambidou, C. Morgan (eds.), *Interpreting the Seventh Century BC: Tradition and Innovation*, Oxford 2017, pp. 38-46.

Batović 1980 = Š. Batović, *L'età del Bronzo Recente sulla costa orientale dell'Adriatico*, *Godišnjak*, 18, 1980, pp. 52-62; pls. I-XVIII.

Bats, D'Agostino 1998 = M. Bats, B. D'Agostino, *Euboica: L'Eubea e la presenza euboica in Calcidica e in Occidente*, Naples 1998.

Berlingò 1986 = I. Berlingò, *La necropoli arcaica di Policoro in contrada Madon- nelle*, in A. De Siena, M. Tagliente (eds.), *Siris-Polieion. Fonti letterarie e nuova documentazione archeologica*, Atti Incontro di Studi (Policoro, 8-10 June 1984), Galatina 1986, pp. 117-127, pls. 9-24.

Berlingò 1993 = I. Berlingò, *Le necropoli di Siris*, in *Bollettino d'Archeologia*, 22, 1993, pp. 1-21.

Berlingò 2000 = I. Berlingò, *Hydriai a Siris*, in I. Berlingò, H. Blanck, F. Cordano, P. G. Guzzo, M. C. Lentini (eds.), *Damarato. Studi di antichità classica offerti a Paola Pelagatti*, Milan 2000, pp. 69-75.

Berlingò 2005 = I. Berlingò, *Policoro (Matera). La necropoli arcaica sud-occidentale di Siris (in proprietà Schirone)*, in *Notizie degli Scavi di Antichità*, (2004- 2005), 2007, pp. 329-379.

Berlingò 2016 = I. Berlingò, *La necropoli arcaica sud-occidentale di Siris (in proprietà Schirone). Scavi 1976-77*, in *SIRIS. Studi e ricerche della Scuola di Specializzazione in Beni Archeologici di Matera*, 16, 2016, pp. 183-203.

Berlingò 2017 = I. Berlingò, *La necropoli arcaica occidentale di Policoro in loc. Madonnelle. Scavi 1977-80*, in *SIRIS. Studi e ricerche della Scuola di Specializzazione in Beni Archeologici di Matera*, 17, 2017, pp. 107-148.

Bettelli 2002 = M. Bettelli, *Italia meridionale e mondo miceneo. Ricerche su di na- miche di acculturazione e aspetti archeologici, con particolare riferimento ai versanti adriatico e ionico della penisola italiana*, Florence 2002.

Bianco 1985 = S. Bianco, *Le vallate dell'Agri e del Sinni: territorio e ambiente*, in S. Bianco, M. Tagliente (eds.), *Il Museo Nazionale della Siritide di Policoro*, Bari 1985, pp. 9-12.

Bianco 1990 = S. Bianco, *Le necropoli enotrie della Basilicata meridionale*, in *Bollettino di Archeologia*, 1-2, 1990, pp. 7-16.

Bianco 1996 = S. Bianco, *L'età del Ferro. La produzione e la circolazione dei beni*, in Bianco et al. 1996 = S. Bianco, A. Bottini, A. Pontrandolfo, A. Russo Tagliente, E. Setari (eds.), *I Greci in Occidente. Greci, Enotri e Lucani nella Basilicata meridionale*, Exhibition catalogue (Policoro, 4 May 1996), Naples 1996, pp. 31-44.

BIANCO 1999A = S. BIANCO, *La prima Età del Ferro*, in D. Adamesteanu (ed.), *1. L'Antichità*, in G. DE ROSA, A. CESTARO (eds.), *Storia della Basilicata*, Rome-Bari 1999, pp. 137-182.

BIANCO 1999B = S. BIANCO (ed.), *Il Museo Nazionale della Siritide di Policoro*, Bari 1999.

BIANCO 1999C = S. BIANCO, *Tursi-Contrada Castello e Cozzo San Martino*, in S. T. Levi (ed.), *Produzione e circolazione della ceramica nella Sibaritide protostorica. I. Impasto e dolii*, Florence 1999, pp. 54-56.

BIANCO 2000 = S. BIANCO, *La necropoli enotria di contrada San Vito*, in Vv.Aa., *Nel cuore dell'Enotria. La necropoli italica di Guardia Perticara*, Exhibition catalogue (Viterbo, 20 October 2000 - 21 January 2001), Rome 2000, pp. 23-28, 47-61.

BIANCO 2001 = S. BIANCO, *Armi e armati nella prima età del ferro*, in Vv.Aa, *Genti in arme. Aristocrazie guerriere della Basilicata antica*, Exhibition catalogue (Rome, 5 July-21 October 2001), Rome 2001, pp. 17-22.

BIANCO 2002 = S. BIANCO, *Immagine e mito nel mondo enotrio*, in Vv.Aa, *Immagine e mito nella Basilicata antica*, Exhibition catalogue (Potenza, December 2002-March 2003), Venosa 2002, pp. 63-72.

BIANCO 2005A = S. BIANCO, *L'ambra nelle vallate della Basilicata ionica*, in Vv.Aa, *Magie d'ambra. Amuleti e gioielli della Basilicata antica*, Exhibition catalogue (Potenza, 2 December 2005-15 March 2006), Lavello 2005, pp. 85-109.

BIANCO 2005B = S. BIANCO, *Guardia Perticara, Contrada San Vito, Tomba 157. III.144. Modello fittile di casa* (Catalogue entry page), in S. SETTIS, M. C. PARRA (eds.), *MAGNA GRÆCIA. Archeologia di un sapere*, Exhibition catalogue (Catanzaro, 19 June-31 October 2005), Milan 2005, p. 396.

BIANCO 2011 = S. BIANCO, *Enotria. Processi formativi e comunità locali. La necropoli di Guardia Perticara*, Lagonegro 2011.

BIANCO 2012A = S. BIANCO, *Presenze insediative indigeni e 'protocoloniali' nell'area del presidio ospedaliero. Nota preliminare*, in M. OSANNA, G. ZUCHTRIEGEL (eds.), ΑΜΦΙ ΣΙΡΙΟΣ ΡΟΑΣ. *Nuove ricerche su Eraclea e la Siritide*, Venosa 2012, pp. 45-67.

BIANCO 2012B = S. BIANCO, *Guardia Perticara (PZ). I modelli fittili in forma di cofanetto provenienti dalla necropoli enotria di contrada San Vito*, in M. OSANNA, V. CAPOZZOLI (eds.), *Nuove ricerche nell'anaktoron di Torre di Satriano*, Atti terzo e quarto convegno di studi su Torre di Satriano (Tito, 16-17 October 2009; 29-30 September 2010), Venosa 2012, pp. 205-264.

BIANCO 2020 = S. BIANCO, *L'acropoli di Chiaromonte: la facies enotria tra X/IX e V secolo a.C.*, in S. BIANCO, A. DE SIENA, D. MANCINELLI, A. PREITE (eds.), *Chiaromonte. Un centro italico tra archeologia e antropologia storica. Studi in memoria di Luigi Viola*, Venosa 2020, pp. 90-131.

BIANCO, DE SIENA 1982 = S. BIANCO, A. DE SIENA, *Termitito*, in L. VAGNETTI (ed.), *Magna Grecia e mondo miceneo. Nuovi documenti*, Taranto 1982, pp. 69-96.

BIANCO, GIARDINO 2010 = S. BIANCO, L. GIARDINO, *Forme e processi di urbanizzazione e di territorializzazione nella fascia costiera ionica tra i fiumi Sinni e Basento*, in *Alle origini della Magna Grecia. Mobilità, migrazioni, fondazioni*, Atti L Convegno di Studi sulla Magna Grecia (Taranto, 1-4 October 2010), Taranto 2012, pp. 609-642.

BIANCO, PREITE 2014 = S. BIANCO, A. PREITE, *Identificazione degli Enotri: fonti e metodi interpretativi*, in *Problemi d'identità nell'Italia preromana: workshop di metodologia*, Conference Proceedings (Rome, 28 June 2013), in *Mélanges de l'École française de Rome*, 126, 2, 2014. https://journals.openedition.org/mefra/2438

BIANCO, PREITE 2016 = S. BIANCO, A. Preite, *La media valle dell'Agrivalle del Sauro*, in A. Preite (ed.), *Energia e Patrimonio culturale in Basilicata e Puglia*, Villa D'Agri 2016, pp. 161-176.

BIANCO, TAGLIENTE 1993 = S. BIANCO, M. TAGLIENTE (eds.), *Il Museo Nazionale della Siritide di Policoro. Archeologia della Basilicata meridionale*, Exhibition Catalogue, Bari 1993.

BIANCO, AFFUSO, PREITE 2021 = S. BIANCO, A. AFFUSO, A. PREITE, *Gli Enotri della Basilicata sud-occidentale. L'evoluzione comparata del diadema copricapo di bronzo*, in G. MITTICA, C. COLELLI, A. LAROCCA, F. LAROCCA (eds.), *Dal Pollino all'Orsomarso. Ricerche archeologiche tra Ionio e Tirreno*, Atti Giornate Internazionali di Archeologia, 2 (San Lorenzo Bellizzi, 4-6 October 2019), *Analecta Romana Instituti Danici*, Supplement LVI, Vols. I-II, Rome 2021, pp. 131-143, 489-499.

BIANCO, PREITE (in press) = S. BIANCO, A. PREITE, *L'orizzonte chonioenotrio tra Agri e Sinni: dinamiche di sviluppo e forme di distinzione sociale*, in *Tra Bradano e Sinni: Greci e popolazioni locali nell'arco jonico (VIII-V sec. a.C.)*, Atti LVI Convegno di Studi sulla Magna Grecia (Taranto, 29 September-1 October 2016), in press.

BIANCO, AFFUSO, PREITE (in press) = S. BIANCO, A. AFFUSO, A. PREITE, *Evidenze archeologiche pre-protostoriche nella valle del Sauro (Basilicata)*, in Atti LV Riunione Scientifica dell'Istituto Italiano di Preistoria e Protostoria della Basilicata (Matera, 6-10 April 2022), in press.

BIANCO, COLELLI, PREITE (in press) = S. BIANCO, C. COLELLI, A. PREITE, *Dal Basento al Crati: l'immagine della donna nella cultura chonia (IX-VIII secolo a.C.)*, in Atti LV Riunione Scientifica Preistoria e Protostoria della Basilicata (Matera, 6-10 April 2022), in press.

Bianco et al. 1996 = S. Bianco, A. Bottini, A. Pontrandolfo, A. Russo Tagliente, E. Setari (eds.), *I Greci in Occidente. Greci, Enotri e Lucani nella Basilicata meridionale*, Exhibition catalogue (Policoro, 4 May 1996), Naples 1996.

Bianco Peroni 1970 = V. Bianco Peroni, *Le spade nell'Italia Continentale*, in *Prähistorische Bronzefunde*, IV, 1, München 1979.

Bianco Peroni 1979 = V. Bianco Peroni, *I rasoi nell'Italia Continentale*, in *Prähistorische Bronzefunde*, VIII, 2, München 1979.

Bolla 2021 = M. Bolla, *Animali di bronzo del Museo Archeologico al Teatro Romano di Verona*, Memorie del Museo Civico di Storia Naturale di Verona. 2, Serie Scienze dell'Uomo, 14, Verona 2021.

Bottini 1984 = A. Bottini, *L'attività archeologica in Basilicata nel 1984*, in *Magna Grecia, Epiro e Macedonia*, Atti XXIV Convegno di Studi sulla Magna Grecia (Taranto, 5-10 October 1984), Naples 1985, pp. 497-511, pls. XXVI-XXXI.

Bottini 1985 = A. Bottini, *L'attività archeologica in Basilicata - 1985*, in *Neapolis*, Atti XXV Convegno di Studi sulla Magna Grecia (Taranto, 3-7 October 1985), Naples 1988, pp. 457-471; pls. LIV-LIX.

Bottini 1993 = A. Bottini, *L'attività archeologica in Basilicata*, in *Magna Grecia Etruschi Fenici*, Atti XXXIII Convegno di Studi sulla Magna Grecia (Taranto, 8-13 October 1993), Naples 1996, pp. 695-709; pls. XLIX-LII.

Bottini 1995 = A. Bottini, *L'attività archeologica in Basilicata nel 1995*, in *Eredità della Magna Grecia*, Atti XXXV Convegno di Studi sulla Magna Grecia (Taranto, 6-10 October 1995), Naples 1998, pp. 629-638.

Bottini 1997 = A. Bottini, *Identità e confini etnico-culturali: l'Italia meridionale*, in *Confini e frontiera nella grecità d'Occidente*, Atti XXXVII Convegno di Studi sulla Magna Grecia (Taranto, 3-6 October 1997), Taranto 1999, pp. 307-326.

Bottini 2000 = A. Bottini, *Kestos himas poikilos*, in *Ostraka*, 9, 2000, pp. 273-278.

Bottini 2007 = A. Bottini, *Re e dinasti italici: il problema della documentazione archeologica*, in P. Scarpi, M. Zago (eds.), *Regalità e forme di potere nel Mediterraneo antico*, Conference Proceedings (Padua, 6-7 February 2004), Padua 2007, pp. 137-155.

Bottini 2016a = A. Bottini, *Popoli anellenici in Basilicata, mezzo secolo dopo*, in M. L. Marchi (ed.), *Identità e conflitti tra Daunia e Lucania preromane*, Pisa 2016, pp. 7-50.

Bottini 2016b = A. Bottini, *Italici e Greci nella Basilicata meridionale, dalla fondazione di Sibari a quella di Metaponto*, in *Atti e Memorie della Società Magna Grecia*, Series V, I, 2016, pp. 139-150.

Bottini 2020 = A. Bottini, *Vasi, strumenti ed armi in metallo*, in S. Bianco, A. De Siena, D. Mancinelli, A. Preite (eds.), *Chiaromonte. Un centro italico tra archeologia e antropologia storica. Studi in memoria di Luigi Viola*, Venosa 2020, pp. 138-153.

Bottini 2023 = A. Bottini, *L'instrumentum domesticum di produzione etrusca presso le compagini indigene dell'attuale Basilicata*, in A. C. Montanaro (ed.), *Vasi di bronzo etruschi in Italia: produzioni regionali e diffusione tra le popolazioni italiche. Contesti d'uso, aspetti ideologici e tecnologici*, in *MEDITERRANEA. Studi e ricerche sul Mediterraneo antico*, 4, 2023, pp. 447-470.

Bottini, Costanzo, Preite 2018 = A. Bottini, D. Costanzo, A. Preite, *Chiaromonte: spazio funerario e struttura sociale di una comunità enotria*, in *Ostraka*, 27, 2018, pp. 5-21.

Bottini et al. 2019 = A. Bottini, R. Graells i Fabregat, M. Vullo, *Metaponto tombe arcaiche della necropoli nord-occidentale*, Venosa 2019.

Botto 2015 = M. Botto, *Ripensando i contatti fra Sardegna e Penisola iberica all'alba del I millennio a.C. Vecchie e nuove evidenze*, in *Revista Onoba*, 3, 2015, pp. 171-203.

Braccesi 2010 = L. Braccesi, *Sulle rotte di Ulisse. L'invenzione della geografia omerica*, Rome-Bari 2010.

Bruno 2018 = S. Bruno, *Dinamiche di popolazione e rituali funerari. Necropoli a enchytrismos e a cremazione nella Sicilia nord-orientale e orientale dell'età del Bronzo*, PhD thesis XXX cycle, University of Messina - Department of Ancient and Modern Civilisations. http://hdl.handle.net/11570/3130732, consulted on 19.07.2024

Brunn 1858 = H. Brunn, *Notizie intorno alle collezioni di antichità dei sigg. Amati a Potenza e Fittipaldi ad Anzi di Basilicata*, Rome 1853.

Buranelli 1985 = F. Buranelli, *L'Urna Calabresi di Cerveteri*, in *Studia Archaeologica*, 41, Rome 1985.

Caputo, Cerzoso 2024 = F. Caputo, M. Cerzoso, *La tessitura*, in M. Cerzoso (ed.), *Enotri*, Soveria Mannelli 2024, pp. 85-87.

Carancini 1975 = L. Carancini, *Gli spilloni nell'Italia continentale*, in *Prähistorische Bronzefunde*, VIII, 2, München 1975.

Cavagnera 1995 = L. Cavagnera, *Ceramica protocorinzia d'importazione e d'imitazione*, in *Ricerche archeologiche all'Incoronata di Metaponto. 3. L'oikos greco del saggio S. Lo scavo e i reperti*, Milan 1995, pp. 35-40.

Cerzoso, Vanzetti 2014 = M. Cerzoso, A. Vanzetti (eds.), *Museo dei Bretti e degli Enotri*, Exhibition Catalogue, Soveria Mannelli 2014.

Charalambidou, Morgan 2017 = X. Charalambidou, C. Morgan (eds.), *Interpreting the Seventh Century BC. Tradition and Innovation*, Oxford 2017.

Chiartano 1994 = B. Chiartano, *La necropoli dell'età del ferro dell'Incoronata e di S. Teodoro (Scavi 1978-1985)*, vols. I-II, Galatina 1994.

Chiartano 1996 = B. Chiartano, *La necropoli dell'età del ferro dell'Incoronata e di S. Teodoro (Scavi 1986-1987)*, vol. III, Galatina 1996.

Christou 1964 = C. Christou, *O Neos Amphoreus tes Spartes*, in *Deltion*, 19, A1, 1964, pp. 164-265.

Cipolloni Sampò 1999 = M. Cipolloni Sampò, *L'Eneolitico e l'Età del Bronzo*, in D. Adamesteanu (ed.), *1. L'Antichità*, in G. De Rosa, A. Cestaro (eds.), *Storia della Basilicata*, Rome-Bari 1999, pp. 67-136.

Colelli, Fera 2013 = C. Colelli, A. Fera, *Bronze chalchophones in Southern Italy Iron age: a mark of identity?*, in L. Bombardieri, A. D'Agostino, G. Guarducci, V. Orsi, S. Valentini (eds.), *Identity and Connectivity: Proceedings of the 16th Symposium on Mediterranean Archaeology* (Florence, Italy, 1-3 March 2012), *British Archaeological Reports. International Series*, S2581, Oxford 2013, pp. 823-832.

Colelli, Jacobsen 2013 = C. Colelli, J. K. Jacobsen, *Excavation on the Timpone della Motta. Francavilla Marittima (1991-2004), II, Iron Age Impasto pottery*, Bari, 2013.

Colucci 2002 = R. Colucci, *Catalogo*, in Vv.Aa., *Immagine e mito nella Basilicata antica*, Exhibition catalogue (Potenza, December 2002-March 2003), Lavello 2002, pp. 143-178.

Cossalter, De Faveri 2008 = L. Cossalter, C. De Faveri, *Incoronata di Metaponto: nuovi dati per la conoscenza della cultura materiale nella prima età del ferro*, in M. Bettelli, C. De Faveri, M. Osanna (eds.), *Prima delle colonie. Organizzazione territoriale e produzioni ceramiche specializzate in Basilicata e in Calabria settentrionale ionica nella prima età del ferro*, Conference Proceedings (Matera, 20-21 November 2007), Venosa 2009, pp. 75-109.

Coudin 2009 = F. Coudin, *Les laconiens et la Méditerranée à l'époque archaïque*, Naples 2009.

Coulie 2013 = A. Coulie, *La céramique grecque aux époques géometrique et orientalisante: XIe-VIe siècles avant J.-C.*, vol. I, Paris 2013.

Cracolici, D'Onghia 2023 = V. Cracolici, P. D'Onghia, *Stamnos* (Catalogue entry page), in C. Greco, F. Frisone (eds.), *Sicilia//Grecia//Magna Grecia. E dunque, quello che cercavo, sono (Odisseo Elitis)*, Exhibition catalogue (Palermo, 20 December 2023-31 March 2024), Soveria Mannelli 2023, p. 28.

Damgaard Andrsen, Winge Horsnæns 2002 = H. Damgaard Andrsen, H. Winge Horsnæns, *Terracotta house models from Basilicata*, in A. Rathje, M. Nielsen, B. Bundsgaard Rasmussen (eds.), *Pots for the living - pots for the dead*, in *Acta Hyperborea*, 9, 2002, pp. 101-126.

D'Agostino 1996 = B. D'Agostino, *La necropoli e i rituali della morte*, in S. Settis (ed.), *I Greci. Storia, cultura, arte, società*, vol. II. *Una storia greca*, 1, *Formazione*, Turin 1996, pp. 435-470.

Denti 2009 = M. Denti, *Un contesto produttivo enotrio della prima metà del VII secolo a.C. all'Incoronata*, in M. Bettelli, C. De Faveri, M. Osanna (eds.), *Prima delle colonie. Organizzazione territoriale e produzioni ceramiche specializzate in Basilicata e in Calabria settentrionale ionica nella prima età del ferro*, Conference Proceedings (Matera, 20-21 November 2007), Venosa 2009, pp. 111-138.

Denti 2012 = M. Denti, *Potiers oenôtres et grecs dans un espace artisanal du VIIe siècle avant J.-C. à l'Incoronata*, in A. Esposito, G. Sanidas (eds.), *'Quartiers' artisanaux en Grèce ancienne: une perspective méditerranéenne*, Villeneuve d'Ascq 2012, pp. 233-256.

Denti 2014 = M. Denti, *Rites d'abandon et opérations d'oblitération « conservative » à l'âge du Fer*, in *L'objet rituel. Méthodes et concepts croisés - The Ritual Object. Differing Concepts and Methods*, *Revue de l'histoire des religions*, 231, 4, 2014, pp. 699-727.

Denti 2016 = M. Denti, *Gli Enotri - e i Greci- sul Basento. Nuovi dati sul Metapontino in età proto-coloniale*, in L. Donnellan, V. Nizzo, G.J. Burgers (eds.), *Contexts of Early Colonization, Acts of the conference: Contextualizing Early Colonization. Archaeology, Sources, Chronology and Interpretative Models between Italy and the Mediterranean* (Rome, 21-23 June, 2012), vol. I, Rome 2016, pp. 223-235.

Denti 2017 = M. Denti, *Topographie et fonction des sols, des fosses, des structures bâties : les résultats des campagnes de fouille de 2015 et 2016 à Incoronata*, in *Chronique des activités archéologiques de l'École française de Rome, Italie du Sud 2017*. https://journals.openedition.org/cefr/1781

Denti 2018 = M. Denti, *Aegean Migrations and the Indigenous Iron Age Communities on the Ionian Coast of Southern Italy. Sharing and Interaction Phenomena*, in E. Gailledrat, R. Plana-Mallart, M. Dietler (eds.), *The emporion in the ancient *western Mediterranean: trade and colonial encounters from the Archaic to the Hellenistic period*, Montpellier 2018, pp. 207-217.

Denti 2024 = M. Denti, *La ceramica greca figurata di Incoronata e della costa io- nica dell'Italia meridionale nel VII secolo a.C. Pittori egei, iconografie eroiche, contesti rituali, mondo indigeno. Incoronata 1*, CNRS - Collection du Centre Jean Bérard 58, Naples 2024.

De Faveri 2005 = C. De Faveri, *Incoronata di Pisticci. III.103 Aryballos globulare* (Catalogue entry page), in S. Settis, M. C. Parra (eds.), *MAGNA GRÆCIA. Archeologia di un sapere*, Exhibition catalogue (Catanzaro, 19 June-31 October 2005), Milan 2005, p. 390.

De Palma 1987 = G. De Palma, *Interventi conservativi e contributi metodologici al microscavo della tomba 110 di Chiaromonte*, in *Poseidonia-Paestum*, Atti XXVII Convegno di Studi sulla Magna Grecia (Taranto-Paestum, 9-15 October 1987), Naples 1992, pp. 690-695.

De Siena 1986 = A. De Siena, *Termitito*, in M. Marazzi, S. Tusa, L. Vagnetti (eds.), *Traffici micenei nel Mediterraneo*, Taranto 1986, pp. 41-54.

De Siena 1990 = A. De Siena, *Contributi archeologici alla definizione della fase precoloniale del Metapontino*, in *Bollettino Storico della Basilicata*, 6, 1990, pp. 71-88.

De Siena 1996 = A. De Siena, *Metapontino: strutture abitative ed organizzazione territoriale prima della fondazione della colonia achea*, in F. D'Andria, K. Mannino (eds.), *Ricerche sulla casa in Magna Grecia e in Sicilia*, Galatina 1996, pp. 161-195.

De Siena 1999 = A. De Siena, *La colonizzazione achea del Metapontino*, in D. Adamesteanu (ed.), *1. L'Antichità*, in G. De Rosa, A. Cestaro (eds.), *Storia della Basilicata*, Rome-Bari 1999, pp. 211-294.

De Siena 2002 = A. De Siena, *Tra Metaponto e Siris: il mito nel mondo greco arcaico*, in Aa.Vv. *Immagine e mito nella Basilicata antica*, Exhibition catalogue (Potenza, December 2002-March 2003), Lavello 2002, pp. 35-46.

De Siena, Giardino 1999 = A. De Siena, L. Giardino, *La costa ionica dall'età del ferro alla fondazione delle colonie: forme e sviluppi insediativi*, in M. Barra Bagnasco, E. De Miro, A. Pinzone (eds.), *Magna Grecia e Sicilia. Stato degli studi e prospettive di ricerca*, Conference Proceedings (Messina, 2-4 December 1996), Rome 1999, pp. 23-38.

De Siena, Preite 2016 = A. De Siena, A. Preite, *Il Metapontino*, in A. Preite (ed.), *Energia e Patrimonio culturale in Basilicata e Puglia*, Villa D'Agri 2016, pp. 193-257.

De Siena, Tagliente 1986 = A. De Siena, M. Tagliente (eds.), *Siris-Polieion. Fonti letterarie e nuova documentazione archeologica*, Atti Incontro di Studi (Policoro, 8-10 June 1984), Galatina 1986.

Donnellan, Nizzo, Burgers 2016 = L. Donnellan, V. Nizzo, G.-J. Burgers (eds.), *Contexts of Early Colonization*, Acts of the conference: Contextualizing Early Colonization. Archaeology, Sources, Chronology and Interpretative Models between Italy and the Mediterranean (Rome, 21-23 June, 2012), vol. I, Rome 2016

Dunbabin 1948 = T. J. Dunbabin, *The Western Greeks. The History of Sicily and South Italy from the Foundation of the Greek Colonies to 480 B.C.*, Oxford 1948.

Ferrante 2022 = N. Ferrante, *La tessitura a Mozia: nuove evidenze*, in *Vicino Oriente*, XXVI, 2022, 2023, pp. 267-294. https://www.vicino-oriente-journal.it/index.php/vicino-oriente/article/view/299, consulted on 14.06.2024.

Finley, Lepore 2000 = M. I. Finley, E. Lepore, *Le colonie degli antichi e dei moderni*, Rome 2000.

Fischer 1990 = J. Fischer, *Zu einer griechischen Kline und weiteren Südimporten aus dem Fürstengrabhügel Grafenbühl, Asperg, Kr. Ludwigsburg*, in *Germania*, 68, 1, 1990, pp. 115-127.

Frey 1991 = O. H. Frey, *Eine Nekropole der Frühen Eisenzeit bei Santa Maria d'Anglona*, Galatina 1991.

Giangiulio 2021 = M. Giangiulio, *Magna Grecia. Una storia mediterranea*, Rome 2021.

Giardino 2010 = L. Giardino, *Forme abitative indigene alla periferia delle colonie greche. Il caso di Policoro*, in H. Tréziny (ed.), *Grecs et Indigene de la Catalogne à la mer Noire*, Actes des rencontres du programme européen Ramses2 (2006- 2008), Bibliothèque d'Archéologie Méediterranéenne et Africaine, 3, Aix-en-Pro- vence 2010, pp. 349-369.

Giardino, De Siena 1999 = L. Giardino, A. De Siena, *Metaponto*, in E. Greco (ed.), *La città greca antica*, Rome 1999, pp. 329-363.

Greco 2005 = E. Greco, *Dalla Grecia all'Italia: movimenti antichi, tradizioni moderne e qualche revisionismo recente*, in S. Settis, M. C. Parra (eds.), *MAGNA GRÆCIA. Archeologia di un sapere*, Exhibition catalogue (Catanzaro, 19 June-31 October 2005), Milan 2005, pp. 58-63.

Greco, Lombardo 2010 = E. Greco, M. Lombardo, *La colonizzazione greca: modelli interpretativi nel dibattito attuale*, in *Alle origini della Magna Grecia. Mobilità, migrazioni, fondazioni*, Atti L Convegno di Studi sulla Magna Grecia (Taranto, 1-4 October 2010), Taranto 2012, pp. 35-60.

Greco, Rizakis 2019 = E. Greco, A. D. Rizakis 2019 (eds.), *Gli Achei in Grecia e in Magna Grecia. Nuove scoperte e nuove prospettive*, Atti Convegno (Aigion, 12-13 dicembre 2016), *Annuario della Scuola archeologica italiana di Atene*, Supplement, 3, Atene 2019.

Guzzo 1994 = P. G. Guzzo, *Oreficerie della Lucania antica*, in *Bollettino storico della Basilicata*, 10, 1994, pp. 25-48, figs. 1-54.

Guzzo 2008 = P. G. Guzzo, *Metaponto, località Crucinia, proprietà Giacovelli. Oreficerie ornamentali dalla tomba 238 in località Crucinia*, in *Bollettino d'Arte*, 143, 2008, pp. 15-26.

Hodos 2006 = T. Hodos, *Local responses to colonisation in the Iron Age Mediterranean*, London-New York 2006.

Horden, Purcell 2000 = P. Horden, N. Purcell, *The corrupting sea: a study of Mediterranean history*, London 2000.

Hurst, Owen 2005 = H. Hurst, S. Owen, *Ancient Colonizations. Analogy, Similarity & Difference*, London 2005.

Ignatiadou 2012 = D. Ignatiadou, *La Sacerdotessa di Sindos*, in N. C. Stampolidis, M. Yannopoulou (eds.), *'Principesse' del Mediterraneo all'alba della Storia*, Exhibition catalogue (Athens, 13 December 2012-8 May 2013), Athens 2012, pp. 388-411.

Knapp, van Dommelen 2011 = B. Knapp, P. van Dommelen, *Material Connections in the Ancient Mediterranean. Mobility, Materiality and Mediterranean Identities*, London-New York 2011.

Lafli, Buora 2006 = E. Lafli, M. Buora, *Fibulae from Cilicia (southern Turkey)*, in *Rivista di archeologia*, 30, 2006, pp. 37-46.

Lane Fox 2010 = R. Lane Fox, *Travelling Heroes: In the Epic Age of Homer*, It. trans. *Eroi viaggiatori. I Greci e i loro miti nell'età epica di Omero*, Turin 2010.

Lattanzi 1981 = E. Lattanzi, *L'attività archeologica in Basilicata nel 1981*, in *Megale Hellas*, Atti XXI Convegno di Studi sulla Magna Grecia (Taranto, 2-5 October 1981), Naples 1983, pp. 259-283; pls. XXXVII-XLI.

Lemos, Kotsonas 2020 = I. S. Lemos, A. Kotsonas (eds.), *The Archaeology of Early Greece and the Mediterranean*, Oxford 2020.

Lippolis, Parisi 2010 = E. Lippolis, V. Parisi, *La ricerca archeologica e le manifestazioni rituali tra metropoli e apoikiai*, in *Alle origini della Magna Grecia. Mobilità, migrazioni, fondazioni*, Atti del L Convegno di Studi sulla Magna Grecia (Taranto, 1-4 October 2010), Taranto 2012, pp. 421-470.

Lyons, Papadopoulos 2002 = C. L. Lyons, J. K. Papadopoulos *The archaeology of colonialism*, Los Angeles 2002.

Lomas 2004 = K. Lomas (ed.), *Greek Identity in the Western Mediterranean: Papers in Honour of Brian Shefton*, Leiden 2004.

Lombardo 1983 = M. Lombardo, *Polieion e il Basento*, in *Attività Archeologica in Basilicata. Studi in Onore di Dinu Adamesteanu*, Galatina 1983, pp. 59-75.

Lombardo 1986 = M. Lombardo, *Siris-Polieion: fonti letterarie, documentazione archeologica e problemi storici*, in A. De Siena, M. Tagliente (eds.), *Siris-Polieion. Fonti letterarie e nuova documentazione archeologica*, Conference Proceedings (Policoro, 8-10 June 1984), Galatina 1986, pp. 55-86.

Lombardo 1998 = M. Lombardo, *Siri e Metaponto: esperienze coloniali e storia sociale*, in *Siritide e Metapontino. Storie di due territori coloniali*, Conference Proceedings (Policoro, 31 October-2 November 1991), Naples 1998, pp. 45-65.

Lombardo 1999 = M. Lombardo, *Profughi e coloni dell'Asia Minore in Magna Grecia (VII-V sec. a.C.)*, in *Magna Grecia e Oriente mediterraneo prima dell'età ellenistica*, Atti XXXIX Convegno di Studi sulla Magna Grecia (Taranto, 1-5 October 1999), Napoli 2000, pp. 189-276

Lombardo 2001 = M. Lombardo, *Pema Iapygessi: Rapporti con gli Iapigi e aspetti dell'identità di Taranto*, in *Taranto e il Mediterraneo*, Atti XLI Convegno di Studi sulla Magna Grecia (Taranto, 12-16 October 2001), Naples 2002, pp. 53-279.

Lo Porto 1959-1960 = F. G. Lo Porto, *Ceramica arcaica dalla necropoli di Taranto*, in *Annuario della Scuola archeologica italiana di Atene*, XXVII, 1959-1960, pp. 7-230.

Lo Porto 1967 = F. G. Lo Porto, *Tombe di atleti tarantini*, in *Atti e Memorie della Società Magna Grecia*, VIII, 1967, pp. 33-98.

Lo Porto 1969 = F. G. Lo Porto, *Metaponto. Tombe a tumulo dell'età del Ferro scoperte nel suo entroterra*, in *Notizie degli Scavi di Antichità*, XXIII, 1969, pp. 121-170.

Lo Porto 1970 = F. G. Lo Porto, *Topografia antica di Taranto*, in *Atti e Memorie della Società Magna Grecia*, X, 1970, pp. 343-383.

Lo Porto 1973 = F. G. Lo Porto, *Civiltà indigena e penetrazione greca nella Lucania orientale*, Monumenti Antichi. Accademia Nazionale dei Lincei, 1973.

Lo Porto 1981 = F. G. Lo Porto, *Ricerche e scoperte nell'Heraion di Metaponto*, in *Xenia*, I, 1981, pp. 25-44.

Lo Porto 2004 = F. G. Lo Porto, *Il deposito prelaconico di Borgo Nuovo*, in *Monumenti Antichi. Accademia Nazionale dei Lincei*, 2004.

Lo Schiavo 2010 = F. Lo Schiavo, *Le Fibule dell'Italia meridionale e della Sicilia dall'età del bronzo recente al VI secolo a.C.*, in *Prähistorische Bronzefunde*, XIV, 14, Vols. 1-3, Firenze 2010.

Lubtchanscky 2005 = N. Lubtchanscky, *Le cavalier tyrrhénien. Représentations équestres dans l'Italie archaique*, Rome 2005.

Luppino et alii 2010 = S. Luppino, F. Quondam, M. T. Granese, A. Vanzetti, *Sibaritide: riletture di alcuni contesti funerari di VIII e VII secolo a.C.*, in *Alle origini della Magna Grecia. Mobilità, migrazioni, fondazioni*, Atti L Convegno di Studi sulla Magna Grecia (Taranto, 1-4 October 2010), Taranto 2012, pp. 645-682.

Maaskant Kleibrink 2003 = M. Maaskant Kleibrink, *Dalla lana all'acqua. Culto e identità nell'Athenaion di Lagaria*, Francavilla Marittima-Rossano 2003.

Maggiani 2002 = A. Maggiani, *Una brocchetta bronzea da Vetulonia*, in *Etruria e Sardegna centro-settentionale tra l'età del bronzo finale e l'arcaismo*, in Atti XXI Convegno di studi etruschi ed italici (Sassari- Alghero-Oristano-Torralba, 13-17 October 1998), Pisa- Rome 2002, pp. 411-418.

Maggiulli 2005 = G. Maggiulli, *Rocavecchia (Lecce): materiali egei e di tipo egeo. II.208. Fibula ad arco semplice* (Catalogue entry page), in S. Settis, M. C. Parra (eds.), *MAGNA GRÆCIA. Archeologia di un sapere*, Exhibition catalogue (Catanzaro, 19 June-31 October 2005), Milan 2005, p. 312.

Malkin 2009 = I. Malkin, *Mediterranean Paradigms and Classical Antiquity*, London-New York 2009.

Malkin 2011 = I. Malkin, *A small greek world: Networks in the Ancient Mediterranean*, Oxford 2011.

Malnati 1985 = L. Malnati, *Tombe arcaiche di S. Maria D'Anglona (scavi 1972-1973)*, in *Quaderni di Acme*, IV, 1984, pp. 41-95; pls. I-XXXIII.

Mancinelli 2003 = D. Mancinelli, *Gli incinerati della necropoli di "Vigna Coretti" presso Timmari (Matera), (campagna di scavo 2001)*, in Atti 23° Convegno Nazionale sulla Preistoria – Protostoria – Storia della Daunia (San Severo, 23-24 November 2002), San Severo 2003, pp. 149-152.

Martelli 2012 = I. Martelli, *Women Go Further: Understanding the Handmade Globular Pyxis from Protogeometric Greece to Southern Italy*, in N. C. Stampolidis, A. Kanta, A. Giannikouri (eds.), *ATHANASIA The Earthly, the Celestial and the Underworld in the Mediterranean from the Late Bronze Age to the Early Iron Age*, Actes International Archaeological Conference (Rhodes, 28-31 May 2009), Herakleion 2012, pp. 321-334. https://www.academia.edu/3347416/Women_Go_Further_Understanding_the_ Handmade_Globular_Pyxis_from_Protogeometric_Greece_to_Southern_Italy_ textile_topic, consulted on 19.07.2024

Mastrocinque 1991 = A. Mastrocinque, *L'ambra e l'Eridano (Studi sulla letteratura e sul commercio dell'ambra in età preromana)*, Este 1991.

Mazzei 2010 = M. Mazzei (ed.), *I Dauni. Archeologia dal IX al V secolo a.C.*, Foggia 2010.

Mele 2013 = A. Mele, *Pitagora filosofo e maestro di verità*, Rome 2013.

Mercuri 2004 = L. Mercuri, *Eubéens en Calabre à l'époque archaique. Formes de contacts et d'implantation*, Bibliothèque des Écoles françaises d'Athènes et de Rome, 321, Rome 2004.

Montanaro 2015 = A. C. Montanaro, *Le ambre figurate in Italia meridionale tra VIII e V secolo a.C. Note sui centri di produzione e sulle botteghe*, in *Taras. Rivista di Archeologia* XXXV, 2015, 2016, pp. 35-64.

Nava 1999 = M. L. Nava, *L'attività archeologica in Basilicata nel 1999*, in *Magna Grecia e Oriente mediterraneo prima dell'età ellenistica*, Atti XXXIX Convegno di Studi sulla Magna Grecia (Taranto, 1-5 October 1999), Naples 2000, pp. 675-726; pls. LII-LXVI.

Nava 2001 = M. L. Nava, *L'attività archeologica in Basilicata nel 2001*, in *Taranto e il Mediterraneo*, Atti XLI Convegno di Studi sulla Magna Grecia (Taranto, 12-16 October 2001), Naples 2002, pp. 719-765; pls. LVIII-LXXVIII.

Nava 2002 = M. L. Nava, *L'attività archeologica in Basilicata nel 2002*, in *Ambiente e paesaggio in Magna Grecia*, Atti XLII Convegno di Studi sulla Magna Grecia (Taranto, 5-8 October 2002), Naples 2003, pp. 653-717; pls. XXVII-LV.

Nava 2003 = M. L. Nava, *Aspetti funerari protostorici nella media Valle dell'Ofanto e nel Materano alla luce dei nuovi scavi della Soprintendenza per i Beni Archeologici della Basilicata*, in Atti 23° Convegno Nazionale sulla Preistoria – Proto-storia – Storia della Daunia (San Severo, 23-24 November 2002), San Severo 2003, pp. 127-138, figs. 1-12.

Nava et al. 1998 = M. L. Nava, B. D'Agostino, M. Gras, P. G. Guzzo, G. Siebert, S. Bianco, G. Greco, E. Pica, A. Russo, M. Tagliente, *Tesori dell'Italia del Sud. Greci e Indigeni in Basilicata*, Exhibition catalogue (Strasbourg, 18 June-15 November 1998), Geneva - Milan 1998.

Nava et al. 2008 = M. L. Nava, S. Bianco, P. Macrì, A. Preite, *Appunti per una tipologia della ceramica enotria: le forme vascolari, le decorazioni, le imitazioni, e le importazioni. Lo stato degli studi*, in M. Bettelli, C. De Faveri, M. Osanna (eds.), *Prima delle colonie. Organizzazione territoriale e produzioni ceramiche specializzate in

Basilicata e in Calabria settentrionale ionica nella prima età del ferro, Conference Proceedings (Matera, 20-21 November 2007), Venosa 2009, pp. 264-276.

ORLANDINI 1980 = P. ORLANDINI, *Perirrhanterion fittile arcaico con decorazione a rilievo dagli scavi dell'Incoronata*, in *Attività archeologica in Basilicata 1964-1977. Scritti in onore di Dinu Adamesteanu*, Matera 1980, pp. 175-238.

ORLANDINI 1983 = P. ORLANDINI, *Scavi e scoperte di VIII e VII secolo a.C. in località Incoronata fra Siris e Metaponto*, in *Grecia, Italia e Sicilia nell'VIII e VII secolo a.C.*, Conference Proceedings (Athens, 15-20 October 1979), *Annuario della Scuola Archeologica di Atene e delle Missioni Italiane in Oriente*, 59, Rome 1983, pp. 315-327.

ORLANDINI 1986 = P. ORLANDINI, *Ricerche all'Incoronata*, in *Lo stretto. Crocevia di culture*, Atti XXVI Convegno di Studi sulla Magna Grecia (Taranto-Reggio Calabria, 9-14 October 1986), Naples 1993, pp. 689-691.

ORLANDINI 1987 = P. ORLANDINI, *Scavi all'Incoronata 1987*, in *Poseidonia-Paestum*, Atti XXVII Convegno di Studi sulla Magna Grecia (Taranto-Paestum, 9-15 October 1987), Naples 1992, pp. 688-690, pls. XCVI-XCVIII.

ORLANDINI 1988 = P. ORLANDINI, *Due nuovi vasi figurati di stile orientalizzante dagli scavi dell'Incoronata di Metaponto*, in *Bollettino d'Arte*, 49, 1988, pp. 1-16.

ORLANDINI 1991 = P. ORLANDINI, *Altri due vasi di stile orientalizzante dagli scavi dell'Incoronata di Metaponto*, in *Bollettino d'Arte*, 66, 1991, pp. 1-8.

ORLANDINI 1992 = P. ORLANDINI, *I vasi figurati*, in P. ORLANDINI, G. STEA, A. SAN PIETRO, *Ceramica dipinta di fabbrica coloniale*, in *Ricerche archeologiche all'Incoronata di Metaponto. 2. Dal villaggio indigeno all'emporio greco. Le strutture e i materiali del saggio T*, Milan 1992, pp. 71-82, figs. 183-187.

ORLANDINI 1995 = P. ORLANDINI, *I vasi figurati*, in P. ORLANDINI, G. STEA, M. PIZZO, *Ceramica dipinta di fabbrica coloniale*, in *Ricerche archeologiche all'Incoronata di Metaponto. Scavi dell'Università degli Studi di Milano. Istituto di Archeologia, 3. L'oikos greco del saggio S. Lo scavo e i reperti*, Milan 1992, pp. 57-88, figs. 175-182.

Orlandini 2000 = P. ORLANDINI, *Il grande perirrhanterion*, in *Ricerche archeologiche all'Incoronata di Metaponto. 4. L'oikos greco del grande perirrhanterion nel contesto del saggio G*, Milan 2000, pp. 23-25.

ORLANDINI et alii 1992 = P. ORLANDINI, G. STEA, A. SAN PIETRO, *Ceramica dipinta di fabbrica coloniale*, in *Ricerche archeologiche all'Incoronata di Metaponto. 2. Dal villaggio indigeno all'emporio greco. Le strutture e i materiali del saggio T*, Milan 1992, pp. 71-82.

ORLANDINI et alii 1995 = P. ORLANDINI, G. STEA, M. PIZZO, *Ceramica dipinta di fabbrica coloniale*, in *Ricerche archeologiche all'Incoronata di Metaponto. 3. L'oikos greco del saggio S. Lo scavo e i reperti*, Milan 1995, pp. 57-88.

OSANNA 2012 = M. OSANNA, *Prima di Eraclea: l'insediamento di età arcaica tra il Sinni e l'Agri*, in M. OSANNA, G. ZUCHTRIEGEL (eds.), ΑΜΦΙ ΣΙΡΙΟΣ ΡΟΑΣ. *Nuove ricerche su Eraclea e la Siritide*, Venosa 2012, pp. 17-43.

OSANNA 2014 = M. OSANNA, *The Iron Age in South Italy: Settlement, Mobility and Culture Contact*, in A. B. KNAPP, P. VAN DOMMELEN (eds.), *The Cambridge Prehistory of the Bronze Age and Iron Age Mediterranean*, Cambridge 2014, pp. 230-248.

OSANNA 2016 = M. OSANNA, *Forme insediative e contatti di culture lungo la costa ionica d'Italia meridionale tra i fiumi Basento e Sinni (VIII - VII sec. a.C.)*, in L. DONNELLAN, V. NIZZO, G.-J. BURGERS (eds.), *Contexts of Early Colonization*, Acts of the conference: Contextualizing Early Colonization. Archaeology, Sources, Chronology and Interpretative Models between Italy and the Mediterranean (Rome, 21- 23 June, 2012), vol. I, Rome 2016, pp. 183-197.

OSANNA 2014 = M. OSANNA, *Interazioni e ibridazioni tra Metapontino e Siritide*, in *Ibridazione e integrazione in Magna Grecia*, Atti LIV Convegno di Studi sulla Magna Grecia (Taranto, 25-28 September 2014), Taranto 2017, pp. 385-404.

OSANNA 2024 = M. OSANNA, *Mondo nuovo. Viaggio alle origini della Magna Grecia*, Milan 2024.

OSANNA, PRANDI, Siciliano 2008 = M. OSANNA, L. PRANDI, A. SICILIANO, *Culti greci in Occidente. Fonti scritte e documentazione archeologica, II. Eraclea*, Città di Castello 2008.

OSBORNE, CUNLIFFE 2005 = R. OSBORNE, B. CUNLIFFE (eds.), *Mediterranean Urbanization. 800-600 B.C.*, Oxford 2005.

OWEN 2005 = S. OWEN, *Analogy, Archaeology and Archaic Greek Colonization*, in H. Hurst, S. Owen, *Ancient Colonizations. Analogy, Similarity & Difference*, London 2005, pp. 5-22.

PACCIARELLI 1999 = M. PACCIARELLI, *Torre Galli. La necropoli della prima età del ferro (scavi Paolo Orsi 1922-23)*, Soveria Mannelli 1999.

PREITE 2017 = A. PREITE, *La necropoli protostorica di Timmari: le TAC esplorano il passato. Approfondimento. La necropoli a incinerazione di Timmari. Gli scavi del 1901*, in *MATHERA. Rivista trimestrale di Storia e Cultura del Territorio*, I, n. 2, 2017, pp. 10-17.

PREITE 2020 = A. PREITE, *Chiaromonte: storia delle ricerche e dinamiche di antro- pizzazione pre-protostorica*, in S. BIANCO, A. DE SIENA, D. MANCINELLI, A. PREITE (eds.),

Chiaromonte. Un centro italico tra archeologia e antropologia storica. Studi in memoria di Luigi Viola, Venosa 2020, pp. 56-89.

Quagliati, Ridola 1906 = Q. Quagliati, D. Ridola, *Necropoli arcaica ad incinerazione presso Timmari nel Materano*, in *Monumenti Antichi. Reale Accademia dei Lincei*, XVI, Milan 1906.

Ridola 1901 = D. Ridola, *La Paletnologia nel materano*, in *Bullettino di Paletnologia Italia*, XXVII, 1901, pp. 27-41.

Saltini Semerari 2019 = G. Saltini Semerari, *Calcophones in Context. Gender, Ritual and Rhythm in Early Iron Age Southern Italy*, in *Mitteilungen des Deutschen Archäologischen Instituts, Römische Abteilung*, Band 125, 2019, pp. 23-26, fig. 6.

Settis 1996 = S. Settis (ed.), *I Greci. Storia, cultura, arte, società*, vol. II. *Una storia greca*, tomo 1, *Formazione*, Turin 1996.

Shefton 1979 = B. B. Shefton, *Die "rhodischen" Bronzekannen*, Mainz 1979.

Shefton 2009 = B. B. Shefton, *Oinochoai and Other Etruscan, Italic, and Greek Vessels in Bronze from Trestina*, in F. Lo Schiavo, A. Romualdi (eds.), *I complessi archeologici di Trestina e di Fabbrecce nel Museo archeologico di Firenze*, in *Monumenti Antichi. Accademia Nazionale dei Lincei*, Miscellaneous series, 66, 2009, pp. 107-138.

Snodgrass 1964 = A. Snodgrass, *Early Greek Armour and Weapons*, Edimburgh 1964.

Stea 1999 = G. Stea, *Forme della presenza greca sull'arco ionico della Basilicata: tra emporìa e apoikìai*, in M. Castoldi (ed.), *Koinà: Miscellanea di studi archeologici in onore di Piero Orlandini*, Milan 1999, pp. 49-71.

Tabone 1996 = G. P. Tabone, *Pendagli figurati in bronzo dell'Età del Ferro nei musei lombardi*, in M. Porumb (ed.), *Omaggio a Dinu Adamesteanu*, Cluj-Napoca 1996, pp. 83-100.

Tagliente 1985 = M. Tagliente, *Elementi del banchetto in un centro arcaico della Basilicata (Chiaromonte)*, in *Mélanges de l'École française de Rome*, 97, 1, 1985, pp. 159-191.

Torelli 1988 = M. Torelli, *Le popolazioni dell'Italia antica: società e forme del potere*, in A. Schiavone, A. Momigliano (eds.), *Storia di Roma*, I, Turin 1988, pp. 53-74.

Torelli 2011 = M. Torelli, *Dei e artigiani. Archeologie delle colonie greche d'Occidente*, Rome-Bari 2011.

Vannicelli 2022 = P. Vannicelli, *Aspetti del consolidamento delle poleis in ambito coloniale*, in C. Colombi, V. Parisi, O. Dally, M. Guggisberg, G. Piras, (eds.), *Comparing Greek Colonies. Mobility and settlement consolidation from Southern Italy to the Black Sea (8th-6th Century BC)*, Berlin-Boston 2022, pp. 9-15.

Verčik 2014 = M. Verčik, *Die barbarischen Einflüsse in der griechischen Bewaffnung*, in *Internationale Archaologie*, 125, 2014, pp. 259-264.

Verger 2014 = S. Verger, *Kolophon et Polieion. A propos de quelques objets métalliques archaïques de Policoro*, in *SIRIS. Studi e ricerche della Scuola di Specializzazione in Beni Archeologici di Matera*, 14, 2014, pp. 15-41.

Verger 2016 = S. Verger, *Deux parures archaïques en bronze de type oriental trouvées dans les fouilles de 1970 au temple archaïque de Policoro*, in *SIRIS. Studi e ricerche della Scuola di Specializzazione in Beni Archeologici di Matera*, 16, 2016, pp. 207-214.

Vullo 2012 = M. Vullo, *Produzioni specializzate di età arcaica a Policoro: le coppe a filetti*, in M. Osanna, G. Zuchtriegel (eds.), ΑΜΦΙ ΣΙΡΙΟΣ ΡΟΑΣ. *Nuove ricerche su Eraclea e la Siritide*, Venosa 2012, pp. 69-87.

Wecowski 2014 = M. Wecowski, *The Rise of the Greek Aristocratic Banquet*, Oxford 2014.

Weidig 2021 = J. Weidig, *The Heroic Virtue of the Warrior. The Tomb of the Duce and the Tomb of the Ivory Box of Belmonte Piceno (prov. Fermo / I)*, in G. Bardelli, R. Graells i Fabregat (eds.), *Ancient Weapons. New Research Perspectives on Weapons and Warfare*, Proceedings of the International Conference (Mainz, 20-21 September 2019), Mainz 2021, pp. 71-90.

Yntema 1990 = D. W. Yntema, *The Matt-Painted Pottery of Southern Italy. A general survey of the matt-painted pottery styles of Southern Italy during the final bronze age and the iron age*, Galatina 1990.

Yntema 2013 = D. W. Yntema, *The Archaeology of South-East Italy in the First Millennium BC. Greek and Native Societies of Apulia and Lucania between the 10th and the 1st Century BC*, Amsterdam 2013.

ICCD - Catalogo generale dei Beni Culturali https://catalogo.beniculturali.it/detail/ArchaeologicalProperty/1700085631, consulted on 20.03.2024 https://catalogo.beniculturali.it/detail/ArchaeologicalProperty/1700212008, consulted on 20.03.2024.

Editor in Chief
Roberto Marcucci

Editorial manager
Elena Montani

Graphic design
Rossella Corcione

Editorial staff
Dario Scianetti
Alessia Francescangeli
David Chacon
Giovanni Ligabue

Accounting
Francesco Cagliuso

Logistics
Luigi Filippo Mariani
Sandro Mannelli

Copyright 2024
© «L'ERMA» di BRETSCHNEIDER
Via Marianna Dionigi, 57 - 00193 Roma
70 Enterprise Drive, Suite 2
Bristol (CT), 06010 - USA
lerma@lerma.it
http://www.lerma.it

ISBN 978-88-913-3407-7 (paper)
ISBN 978-88-913-3409-1 (digital)
DOI: 10.48255/9788891334091
CDD 709.01
1. Basilicata - Archeologia

Quality Management Systems (QMS)
UNI EN ISO 9001:2015
Enviromental Management System (EMS)
ISO 14001:2015

All right reserved. No part of this publication may be reproduced, translated, stored in a retrivial system, or trasmitted in any form or by any means, electronic, mechanical, photocopying, recording or otherwise without prior written permission from the publisher.

Printed in September 2024 on behalf of
«L'ERMA» di BRETSCHNEIDER
by CSC Grafica s.r.l. - via A. Meucci, 28
00012 - Guidonia - Rome